Anna Hart is a writer specialising in lifestyle, travel and international culture. She has over ten years' experience writing for *Grazia*, *Vogue*, *Stylist*, *GQ*, *Elle*, the *Guardian*, the *Telegraph*, *The Times*, *Wall Street Journal* and *Condé Nast Traveller*. She was formerly contributing Travel Editor at *Stylist* magazine, and is currently a regular columnist at the *Daily Telegraph* and speaker at events such as Stylist LIVE and WOW at the Southbank centre, and on the radio.

'A beautiful memoir about travel and letting go' Dawn O'Porter, *Sunday Telegraph*

'From Bali to LA, New Zealand to er, Margate, even armchair travellers will get a vicarious thrill from *Departures*' Red

'Stories of growing up via far-flung adventures and eye-opening city breaks are so warm, witty and gorgeously written that it's hard not to find yourself on Skyscanner within half an hour of cracking the book open' *The Pool*

'I read it in one day' Jamie Klingler, *iNews*

'A call to action for women everywhere. Hart writes about the transformative and healin[g] can last way past touchdo[wn]

DEPARTURES

A guide to letting go,
one adventure at a time

ANNA HART

sphere

SPHERE

First published in Great Britain in 2018 by Sphere
This paperback edition published in 2019 by Sphere

1 3 5 7 9 10 8 6 4 2

A CIP catalogue record for this book
is available from the British Library.

ISBN 978-0-7515-7705-1

Typeset in Baskerville by M Rules
Printed and bound in Great Britain by
Clays Ltd, Elcograf S.p.A.

Papers used by Sphere are from well-managed forests
and other responsible sources.

Sphere
An imprint of
Little, Brown Book Group
Carmelite House
50 Victoria Embankment
London EC4Y 0DZ

An Hachette UK Company
www.hachette.co.uk

www.littlebrown.co.uk

This book is dedicated to my mum, Pat,
my dad, Ian, my sister, Naomi and my brother, Peter,
the best travel companions I could
ever have hoped for.

Contents

Introduction

Getting Away From It All

Like many of the world's travel obsessives, I was born some-where worth escaping from, the 'troubled' Belfast of the 1980s and 1990s. The word 'troubles' is a characteristically low-key Northern Irish term for what amounted to decades of political turbulence, paramilitary violence both horrifyingly large scale and revoltingly petty, economic depression and pervasive social gloom. 'The Troubles' sounds more like PMT; not thirteen-year-olds being blown up in chip shops, kneecappings, women being tarred and feathered and hunger strikes in the Maze prison. The Belfast I eagerly abandoned at the age of seventeen is camouflage-coloured in my mind, the slate grey of the skies and the streets forming a backdrop to the green smears of distant hills, a dreary colour palate replicated in the military uniforms on every street corner.

Being from Belfast took me by surprise, because from the age of five until I was twelve I lived on the opposite side of the world, in the steamy, equatorial financial powerhouse of Singapore.

1

It's an irony not lost on me that the most significant journey of my life will always be this move to Singapore, instigated by my Northern Irish parents, who are the best adventure travellers I know. My mum, Patricia, is a relentlessly energetic and fiercely intelligent ophthalmologist, who met my father, Ian, when they were both at Queen's University Belfast. Dad was studying French and German literature, but soon segued into theology, and by the time I was born my ambitious and free-spirited mum had found herself an accidental vicar's wife.

In 1985, my dad spotted an advert in the somewhat niche periodical *Presbyterian Irishman*: an appeal from a Singaporean congregation for an interim pastor and lecturer for a couple of years. I always thought my dad must have felt some sort of spiritual thunderbolt at this moment, but in fact he remembers thinking, 'I really, really hope somebody else answers this advert.' But my dad spotted it in the next issue of *Presbyterian Irishman*. And the next. For my dad, adventure and travel are simply the occasionally unfortunate by-products of doing something important and good, or 'being of use', as he would put it. From 1970 to 1972 Dad taught in a secondary school and teacher training college in Shyogwe, Rwanda, about forty miles south-west of the capital, Kigali. Years later, in 2017, I was sent on a group press trip to Rwanda and Uganda, gorilla-tracking in the Virunga mountain range and Bwindi Impenetrable Forest. I thought this was pretty intrepid until I showed my dad our itinerary, and he went through it methodically, enthusing about what a wonderful time I'd have, but also casually dropping in references to hitchhiking and walking across the Congolese border twice in order to travel from Shyogwe to Kampala in

Uganda after Idi Amin closed the Uganda–Rwanda border in 1971. As a student backpacker, then solo female traveller and eventual travel writer, I've done way more than my fair share of adventuring (I sometimes worry that, to redress the balance, at the age of forty I'll be shoved on to a desk and forced to do cross-stitch while somebody else has their turn at FUN) but I know I'll never, ever out-adventure my father or my mother.

Just as my dad was returning from Rwanda, Mum departed for Tanzania, to spend her summer as a final-year medical student at Kilimanjaro Christian Medical Centre (KCMC) in Moshi. International electives are obviously common practice now, but back in 1973, out of a class of 110, only five students chose to go abroad. Mum went because she wanted to 'experience medicine in a different environment, and to see the changes that medicine makes to the lives of people'. And it changed the course of her career for ever; it was there that she helped out at the eye department, and saw the huge difference that one small speciality, ophthalmology, could make to someone's quality of life. 'A simple procedure gave someone their life back – and their livelihood back – which in Africa means everything,' she said.

A few years later, when I showed up as a baby with the potential to ruin both their lives, they didn't quit on travel, adventure or usefulness. When I was two and my sister Naomi six months old, my parents took us to Yavatmal Province in India for six months, where Mum administered eye drops and Dad taught in a Bible college, Union Biblical Seminary. Dad would never travel purely for the sake of adventure, like I do, along with the rest of my indulgent generation. Mum, meanwhile, combines the wanderlust and curiosity of the incurable romantic with the resourcefulness and can-do positivity of a medic. They are superlative travellers, and I never expect to be as good at travelling as either of them. But it's been a lot of fun trying.

In 1985 they packed our belongings into tea chests and boarded a British Airways flight to Singapore with five-year-old me, three-year-old Naomi and my dinky, big-eyed one-year-old brother, Peter. We got our first taste of that special brand of South East Asian generosity, hospitality and intrinsic cuteness minutes after landing at Changi Airport. Our plane touched down at 2 a.m., but that hadn't stopped most of the congregation from turning up to welcome us in the arrivals hall, with a massive banner reading, 'Katong Presbyterian Church welcomes the Hart Family!' illustrated with two big ♥s and three small ♥s. Peter was bewildered and began to cry. Mum wished she'd brushed her hair as she was draped with flower garlands and dragged into photographs that would adorn the walls of Singapore Presbyterian Church for years. As for me, I was delighted. I'd never seen anything as glossy and futuristic as Changi Airport, which looked to me like something straight out of *The Jetsons*. And I'd never had a banner devoted to me before.

The thing about travelling when you're really young is that because everything is new to you, life in a new country is no newer than life in the old one. It's ALL new. Everything in the world is equally weird. So, when we were small, we adapted quickly to Singaporean life, popping on flip flops instead of plimsolls, being scared of cockroaches instead of daddy-long-legs (a substantial escalation of entomological terror; how we longed for the genteel, reserved, European daddy-long-legs) and eating mangoes instead of apples.

My brother, Peter, was enrolled in a state nursery school. English is the official language of Singapore, but school classes are taught in Mandarin so that Singaporeans grow up bilingual. Peter was soon chattering away in Mandarin and English, and we were all jealous. Naomi and I, being a bit older, went to an international school so that we could actually understand our lessons. Singapore Preparatory School, affectionately known as Singapore Papaya Tree School, was run by a formidable woman named Mrs Barnard. Formidable Englishwomen are something of a feature in Singapore; this was my first real experience of Englishness, and getting the expatriate version was like sipping port instead of wine. The English wear conventions like armour, and I was fascinated by the various rules, traditions and ways of doing things that they had.

Natalia Barnard believed it was her job to instil Britishness in us, her particular brand of Britishness, and the walls around our tiny school marked her personal fiefdom. The books we were handed were all 1950s English mainstays: Enid Blyton's *Malory Towers* and *The Famous Five* series, E. B. White's *Charlotte's Web*, and J. M. Barrie's *Peter Pan*. Neatness was important to Mrs Barnard; sweat was fine, stains were not, and we were expected to wear white cotton socks with our brown sandals. We lived for Wednesdays, aka pancake day, when Lakshmi, a lovely local Malay woman, would fry up crepes on a tiny camping stove under the tree outside, which we could buy for forty cents. The word 'Wednesday' still smells of pancakes to me; every day of the week has its own flavour, and, thirty years on, Wednesday's is fried batter.

It was at SPS that I had my first major literary success, writing the school Christmas play, some sort of Enid Blyton/Roald Dahl mash-up involving animated toys and a bossy frog. At this stage in our lives, all expatriate children in Singapore believed that Santa visited via the rubbish chute, in the worrisome absence of chimneys. This is what expatriate life is like; desperately trying to fit old psychological furniture into a brand new flat hopelessly unsuited to such items.

We only returned to Ireland to visit family twice in seven years; those were the days when international travel cost big. Even phone calls cost big, and we spoke to our grandparents on birthdays and at Christmas. Back in Ireland, well-meaning but heroically ignorant people would ask us what it was like living 'in the jungle'. It's hard, when you're seven, to explain that, in its twenty-five years since gaining independence in 1965, Singapore had become the economic success story of South East Asia, with a state-of-the-art air-conditioned MRT (mass rapid transport) system, soaring skyscrapers and gleaming hospitals. Singapore was a futuristic vision, a sci-fi film set, compared to Ireland at the time; it was plain to me which one of my homes was the sleepy backwater.

It was only when I got a little older, when I made the rookie error of starting to expect something resembling normality from life, rather than non-stop newness and strangeness, that I began to find expatriate life a bit weird. Being an outsider has its advantages, but being an expat needs to be deftly navigated if you don't want to wind up hating the locals, or having the locals hate you, or, worst of all, spending all your time with hateful people from your own country moaning about how things aren't as good as they are back home.

My parents had made the entirely admirable decision not to live in some creepy mock-Tudor expat enclave with a name like 'Folkstone Village', like my best friend, Emma, did. Instead, we lived near the church in Joo Chiat in Katong. Back then it was considered the red-light district, not that I knew any of this when I was a kid, which is a damned shame because I would have delighted in this detail on a daily basis. I was obsessed with hookers as a child, and spent most Sundays at church flicking through the Old Testament looking for prostitutes or other juicy bits. I think I remember Esther being a particularly good chapter.

Anyway! Today, the east coast neighbourhood of Joo Chiat is a designated heritage town and the best place to immerse yourself in Peranakan culture, with pastel-hued heritage two-storey shophouses with ornate facades, intricate motifs and ceramic tiling. Cool cafés now rub up against no-frills eating houses serving Katong *laksa* and *kueh chang* (dumplings), amongst other Nonya treats, and boutique hotels are springing up next to shops where they'll fix your phone for $5.

Today, naturally, I'm thrilled that I can brag to Singaporeans about growing up in Joo Chiat, buying Chiclets from those crumbling shophouses and developing a lifelong taste for *Nyonya bak chang* dumplings. I get instant credit for knowing my way around the streets of Katong rather than the expat shopping hub of Holland Village.

Retrospectively, I'm delighted that I learned to windsurf along with sporty locals at the East Coast Sailing Centre. And above all, I'm glad that my family had mainly Singaporean friends, spending our free time eating satay in hawker centres, attending mass Chinese family gatherings and being genuinely plugged in to the Singaporean community, rather than simply plugged into a computer at an international bank in the CBD (central business district), with your heart and soul remaining elsewhere in the world, and a whitewashed, expat-only social life to prove where your loyalties lie.

But when you're nine, you have shit taste, and just want what your school friends have. I'd found myself a gang of lushly international misfits to hang around with, and with whom I remain Facebook friends, but we were still surrounded by an overwhelming majority of affluent and regularly spoiled expat children. These were the offspring of bankers, entrepreneurs and diplomats, couples who left their kids in the hands of Filipino maids and let them do whatever the hell they wanted to make up for it. And I just wanted to join them, eating fish and chips in the colonial surroundings of the British Club, shopping in Holland Village and going to pool parties in swanky condominiums in Clementi.

Truthfully, I think I'd have been an awkward and oversensitive child whatever the circumstances, but it didn't help my latent security issues that my best friends routinely moved on after a parent's two-year contract in the city ended. Seven years at international school in Singapore made us veterans. Or lingering, lonesome losers, depending on how you wanted to look at it. And, increasingly, the way I wanted to look at things was grim, dark and morose, like a tiny Morrissey.

By the age of eleven I began experiencing panicky episodes and had trouble sleeping, assailed by what I tentatively labelled 'my yucky feelings'. I can see now that this was some form of juvenile depression, anxiety and panic attacks as clumsily assembled by an eleven-year-old. My concerned mum gently introduced me to a child psychologist, and I explained my various anxieties and fears: about how I'd never have a real friend for life because Singapore was just a 'stopping-off place', where friends moved on, leaving gaping, tattered holes in my life. I'd also developed a near-constant dread of something bad happening to my family, who I adored and depended upon so intensely that I felt it was unlikely that the world, this cruel world, would let me keep them. That would be uncharacteristically generous of the world, I felt, because seemingly I wasn't allowed to keep any of my friends. And since my nine-year-old sister wasn't going to get a new job as a pilot in Melbourne, like my departed friend Penny's dad, Naomi's disappearance from my life would necessitate some sort of horror that I pieced together from the newspaper headlines that haunted my overactive mind – a car crash, a sinking ferry, perhaps a rogue ball in a game of rounders. Naomi had secretly been in my list of Top Five Friends ever since I turned seven, although I'd scribble her name out on a near-daily basis. Please, I asked the world, please can I keep her?

I worried that nobody really liked me at school, that they were all busy having pool parties at each other's condominiums and being shitty to their maids while I languished in stupid boring old Joo Chiat, Joo Chiat that would obviously NEVER be cool. I was also intensely concerned about human spontaneous combustion, a charming specialist interest I'd nurtured after coming across the phenomenon in a strange pseudoscientific almanac bought in a budget bookstore. One day my mum peered over my shoulder, perhaps alerted by yet another sharp intake of breath and my look of wide-eyed horror, and promptly chucked 'that rubbishy book' down the garbage chute, where I was sure Santa would find and enjoy it. But she didn't swoop before I'd exhaustively researched my favourite new pet subject. Even today I can rattle off the most notable twentieth-century examples of spontaneous human combustion (SHC) and expound upon Michael Harrison's suggestion that SHC is explained by poltergeist activity. Really, you and I should chat sometime!

I read up on spontaneous combustion until I was so petrified of exploding at some inopportune moment that I tried to persuade my mum to let me sleep in the shower, so I could conveniently extinguish myself with minimal fuss. I thought we should all be sleeping in showers, to be perfectly frank. The danger was real.

Religion, naturally, only made all my anxieties and fears worse. I've always felt like religion functions much like lemon juice on wounded skin, locating those previously unnoticed blemishes on our heart, exacerbating any minor abrasions on our soul. And thanks to Singapore's melting-pot culture, on top of pervasive Protestant guilt I could add terrifying notions of hungry ghosts that needed to be left platefuls of ant-enticing Ritz biscuits or they'd nibble on your soul instead. And evil spirits lurking around in everyday objects like pot plants. And animal reincarnation. I creatively mixed and matched all the most alarming and repressive elements of Hinduism, Buddhism, Islam and the Christian faith, threw in a handful of cockroaches and topped it off with spontaneous combustion, and stirred up this horror stew every night as soon as my hot little head hit the pillow. Sweet dreams.

At this troubled (in the non-Belfast sense) time, my happy place was Changi Airport, also the happy place of many a wearied business traveller. This shiny, air-conditioned Utopia contained a butterfly park, a Swensen's ice cream parlour, countless state-of-the-art moving walkways and a viewing gallery from where we could watch planes take off and land. I think it was perhaps the free air con that most attracted my parents, but Changi became a regular family excursion, just fifteen minutes from our steamy little two-bedroom flat. (Our flat did actually have air con, but it cost a fortune, like everything did for families in the 1980s, so it felt like a luxury that just belonged to condominiums in Clementi, or Changi Airport.) I loved watching the destination flip-board reshuffling to announce exotic destinations: HELSINKI, DELHI, MOSCOW. Airports are found theatres, arenas where relationship dramas unfold, tears are shed and Toblerones are purchased; all human life is here.

I'd gaze in awe at the swishy-haired Singaporean businesswomen, tugging wheelie suitcases across the concourse before boarding flights to Houston. I'd stare at khaki-clad Australian adventurers with battered leather trunks, en route to Nairobi. Surrounded by travellers, my sense of not quite belonging disappeared. As travellers, none of us quite belong, which means we all do.

In 1992, my parents told Naomi, Peter and I that we'd be returning to Belfast imminently. My dad had finally found a suitable replacement pastor for the church, my grandparents were getting older and desperate to see their only grandkids, and I also suspect my mum detected that I was a) a little bit mental and b) on the cusp of adolescence, and if they didn't eject me from the international school system fast, they would wind up with an American teenager on their hands.

Naomi, Peter and I were delighted. We were going home! For years I'd kept my 'flying home drawer' at the ready, a stash of tiny hotel room shampoos and body lotions, an unread 'emergency' Archie comic, and other travel essentials like a light-up yo-yo and snap-on bracelet. Naomi, Peter and I used to play a game in the back of the car, inventively called 'Aeroplane', where we furiously debated what movie we'd watch or what snack we'd order next.

Obviously we were sad to be leaving our Singaporean church friends, our current school friends – although most of them only had another four months on their dad's contract – and our cat, Gingie. But wouldn't it be good to finally feel like we belonged?

'Where the fuck are *you* from?' was the wrinkle-nosed reaction we all got our first day at school in Belfast. No matter how awkwardly Irish we'd felt in Singapore, we soon realised we weren't nearly Irish enough for Ireland. Our tanned skin, mongrel international school accents and tiny giveaways like the fact we lost our minds when we spotted 'cows in the wild' (in Singapore the only cow we saw was in the zoo, okay?) all branded us as outsiders. And as we belatedly came to appreciate, Singapore treated outsiders much more graciously than Belfast did.

Naomi had a particularly rotten time, being bullied by the little twats in her year. I was more fortunate, falling in with a crowd of slightly kooky yet strangely high-status thirteen-year-old girls within the Form 2 social ecosystem. Sarah, Maeve, Wai-Fun, Ellie, Renee, Anna and Munira rather liked my oddball accent, unsuitable tie-dyed clothing bought on a family holiday to Bali, and my amusing unworldliness. (Of course, I *was* worldly. I just wasn't Irelandly.) But even with good friends to help me navigate school, the older I got, and the closer I looked, the stranger Belfast became.

I couldn't get used to the gun-toting security guards at the doors of Boots on Royal Avenue, rifling through my school bag on the way *in*to the store. (On the plus side, their focus on explosive devices entering the building made it piss-easy to shoplift Boots' Natural Collection black cherry lip balm.)

I couldn't help feeling sorry for the miserable-looking twenty-year-old soldiers forced to crouch, in the drizzle, behind telephone boxes and in doorways in the city centre. But I soon learned that it wasn't okay to say this, so I kept my treacherous sympathy to myself. I initially thought the 12 July marches would be like the happy, family-oriented Chinese New Year parade events in Singapore, complete with lion dances and buttered corn. I was bewildered when Munira gently told me that it wasn't okay to look forward to 12 July, that this was a depressing, inevitably violent catwalk devoted to Protestant political posturing.

And it gradually sank in that my country was mainly famous for terrorism. In the 1990s, this was Northern Ireland's big cultural export, what we brought to the world's party. I realised that we wouldn't have the opportunity to drag tourists to the Giant's Causeway, to the beautiful Mourne Mountains, to the Crown Pub. No bugger wanted to come.

Nobody is immune to politics, and in Belfast the depressing political situation sank into us all like damp. It paralysed progress, on a macro-societal level as well as personally, in our everyday lives. Nobody really fancied their chances investing here; you'd have to pay protection money, and employ security guards, and because there was no investment, customers wouldn't have the money to spend in your soon-to-be fire-bombed shop or café anyway. Belfast got its first cappuccino around seven years after the froth was topping mugs in similarly sized cities, such as Glasgow, Birmingham and Dublin.

The Belfast I spent my teenage years in was a once-grand industrial city, with a time-warp small-town mentality. Sticking out at all – by looking different, sounding different or being different – was met with bitter rebukes. The offence of wearing sunglasses on the street would draw choice comments from passers-by, such as 'fuckin' poser'. At fifteen I remember proudly debuting my vintage flared Levi's jeans that I hoped made me look a little bit like Marianne Faithfull. The driver of a passing car wound down his window and bellowed, 'fuckin' hippy'. I was FIFTEEN. All I'd done was stray a few inches beyond socially sanctioned boot-cut denim. And nothing was mocked more robustly than personal ambition. 'Putting someone in their place' or 'taking so-and-so down a peg' was virtually a national sport. 'Pride comes before a fall' was a favourite tutting utterance. What complete fucker thought that one up?

There are a few uninspired but undeniably effective Northern Irish words to describe this very act of passing judgement on others, sneering and radiating disapproval. Such people are either 'slabbering' or 'pass-remarkable', as in they pass way too many remarks. There were lots of pass-remarkable people in Northern Ireland in the 1990s. To me, their presence was greater and more oppressive than the British armed forces. I began to readjust my understanding of the height of civilisation, as a place where people can wear whatever the hell they like without having some wanker shout at them in the street. And perhaps talk about what they'd like to do with their lives, without snorts of derision.

For decades, Singapore has been a place where ambition is kindled, fanned, doused in petroleum. Opportunity exists on every street corner. In contrast, Belfast offered young people very little by way of opportunity. I'd had a paper round when I was fourteen, delivering the *Belfast Newsletter* around south Belfast, but at sixteen I carefully concocted my CV, bigging up my status as a 'founding member of the Victoria College Belfast WWF Club (wildlife, not wrestling)' and GCSE results, printed off twenty copies that I carefully stapled together, and dropped it into twenty chip shops around town. With no luck whatsoever. There were so few jobs going in Belfast that they all had their pick of hotshot applicants with former experience of operating a deep-fat fryer.

I can't work out if it was the pervasive gloom of 1990s Belfast, or purely the Celtic compulsion to get as shitfaced as possible as often as possible, that led to my binge-drinking teenage years. We drank cheap white cider at glamorous locations like MGM (the cinema car park) or Europa (the hotel car park) or occasionally, to give us a break from car parks, Botanics or Cranmore parks. Throwing up behind the bandstand of Cranmore Park was just part of a good night out. I still know all the best spots in the park for fingering.

Finally, six months after my photocopied CV airstrike of all the fast food outlets in town, I got a call from Abrakebabra on Shaftesbury Avenue, a car-jammed thoroughfare dubbed Belfast's 'Golden Mile' in honour of neon-lit shitty nightclubs, chip shops and off-licences. I worked the 10 p.m. to 5 a.m. shift at Abrakebabra in a green polo T-shirt and palm-tree-emblazoned baseball cap declaring, 'Magic Food, Magic Service!', earning £2.75 an hour. Quite a lot of people only worked one shift before quitting, grossed out either by the pay, the endless queues of braying drunkards or the thick layer of lamb grease on their faces by the end of the night. But I plainly have no such standards, and I thought £2.75 an hour was rather wonderful. I could just about earn £25 a weekend, which meant I could save up for the most exciting and glamorous thing imaginable: a weekend away in Dublin with my friends or my boyfriend, Cillian, who had just unforgivably resigned a plumb job at McDonald's in Lisburn. We saved and we saved. Our trip was delayed when I bought myself a £75 black, 1960s-style trench from Warehouse (the first time I made a serious fashion choice on my own and bought it with my own earnings; I still wear it today) but we kept saving. I found a little red retro overnight case in a charity shop to complete the overall look I was going for at the time, which can be described as 'naive and entirely affordable 1960s prostitute en route to Blackpool in the rain', a look I'm not ashamed to admit I regularly reprise at the age of thirty-five.

Finally, we had our funds, and I had my little red suitcase crammed with vintage polyester and M&S opaque tights, so we bought train tickets, lied to our parents about who we were going away with, and set off for Jury's Hotel. We were terrified we'd be turned away at the front desk, for not being old enough, rich enough, or just, well, *enough*. Even fifteen years later, as a travel writer and editor, I still have this sense of not being *enough* when I walk into a hotel lobby. I believe the primary role of all front-of-house staff is to quell the barely concealed imposter syndrome that assails most human beings, and persuade a guest, client, diner or audience member that, yes indeed, they are welcome here.

But the staff of Jury's did not turn us away for being seventeen, or come and chuck us out for being drunk in the middle of the night. And we got to feel like grown-ups. Obviously the main item on our itinerary that weekend was getting drunk and fooling around, but we were also precocious literary dorks and wanted to see the pubs where James Joyce had drunk, wander St Stephen's Green, and pretend, for one glorious weekend, that we were different people. Sophisticated, Dublin-dwelling adults who visited art galleries! Who could have sex without worrying that Cilliain's sister would hear them. With my little red overnight bag, I felt like I was ready for a whole world of adventure, and a whole world of possibilities that were far, far more glamorous than my grey existence in Belfast.

The next weekend, I was back at Abrakebabra, but with a renewed sense of purpose. Money now meant just one thing to me: escape. I already had a Boots lip balm, after all; so my funds could go entirely into travel. Into getting away from it all. Because the greatest ambition you could have in Belfast at that time was to get the hell out.

This book is dedicated to all of us who need to get the hell out. It's about the process of becoming a traveller, and, finally, becoming a good traveller. It's also about how not to travel, the many mistakes I made along the way. It's about the dizzying highs and crashing lows of solo travel. It's about the realities of travel, an unfiltered account rarely found in print or social media. It's about working out why we travel. It's about who we become when we travel. And it's about working out when to stop travelling, and sit still for a moment.

Thank you for sitting still, for a moment, with this book. I wrote it for you.

1

Poland: How to Be a Grown-up

I'd love to begin my travel memoir by declaring that my decision to spend a gap year teaching English in Warsaw was the result of an adolescent fondness for the music of Chopin, my passion for twentieth-century history or my painstakingly accrued appreciation of Warsaw's diverse architectural heritage.

But I'm a completely different person from that, sorry. And I decided to take a gap year purely because I hated the thought of embarking upon Freshers' Week at Glasgow University at the age of seventeen, i.e. too young to get legally shitfaced. I was one year ahead in school, so graduating straight from Victoria College in Belfast to Glasgow University meant doing all my friend-making and amazing-new-life-creating in the cold, sober light of day. As a thoroughly awkward and socially anxious teenager who'd spent the past few years forging fledgling friendships in the fires of flaming sambucas, this was unthinkable. Nobody would like me sober. I didn't even like myself when I was sober.

And I chose Poland because, well, okay, I didn't exactly

choose Poland. It was the only destination with any placements left by the time I got around to applying for a gap year. But, at seventeen, everywhere was new; anywhere but Belfast was an adventure. And anywhere would do, really, to ride out those final, lame-duck months as an illegal drinker. I had no idea how much this year in Poland would change me, kick-starting a lifelong love affair with Eastern Europe, shaping my travel tastes for ever and delivering me back to the UK as not merely a legal adult, but a grown-up.

To raise the couple of grand I needed for my gap year, I worked at an old people's home all summer, literally wiping older people's arses to pay for my trip. This is a brilliant thing to have to do as a seventeen-year-old; I can't recommend it more highly. As it happens, older people have quite nice arses; silken-skinned and pleasingly puckered. The rest of an older person is pretty decent, too. I enjoyed shooting the breeze with sharp-as-a-tack ninety-eight-year-old Mrs Erskine. I loved talking to Miss Kelly about the awards and decorations she'd been given over a lifetime dedicated to medical research. And I enjoyed gently cajoling Mrs Horrocks, who suffered from a pleasant form of dementia which allowed us to chat with her reflection in the mirror as I got her ready for bed; the three of us really got on.

I learned a great deal at Adelaide House. I learned how to stay awake through the tricksy hour of 3–4 a.m. on a night shift, a skill that would soon come in handy at ridiculous all-night parties at university in Glasgow, and has more recently proven useful on press trips with gruelling itineraries, where sleep is tightly rationed. I learned that if you deny a British person a cup of tea served precisely the way they like it, you are essentially denying them their individuality, their autonomy, their very humanity. I learned how to fold hospital corners, how to bake scones and how to chat away merrily regardless of the circumstances, pretending it's not weird that you're drying the underside of someone's tits.

And I like to think that being surrounded by so much age, when I myself had so little age, made me determined not to waste a single year of my life. The people I was caring for really, really knew the value of time, and they gently impressed upon me the importance of not squandering mine.

And now I had my first ever solo adventure abroad! When I told the residents of Adelaide House I would be spending a gap year in Poland, most of them looked at me askance. Belfast in the late 1990s was a relatively grim place, but Warsaw in the late 1990s didn't sound like a vast improvement. Surely I could get a job somewhere jolly, like Marbella or Blackpool?

But over the years I've learned that many of the most reward-ing destinations are the places that other people consider a weird choice. I've come to relish that askance glance, which I now see as a harbinger of a memorable trip. During a recent meeting with the editor of *Suitcase* magazine, I described one of my spe-cialist interests within travel writing as 'places that other people would describe as shitholes'. She diligently scribbled 'shitholes' underneath my other areas of journalistic expertise, including 'cross-country skiing', 'adventure travel', 'budget city hotels', 'Scottish campsites' and 'live–work destinations'.

If I was Lauren Bacall in a 1940s film noir, I guess I'd murmur that I like my cities like I like my men: complex but rewarding, mean but romantic, ungroomed but beguiling. Glasgow, Detroit,

Naples, Marseilles, Belgrade, Manila and São Paulo are all gritty, bad-boy cities that I found myself uncontrollably in lust with, after just one dirty weekend.

On the flight from Belfast to Warsaw, I figured I'd better learn something about my new home for the next six months, and finally got around to reading the history chapter in my trusty *Rough Guide*. Even today, in the internet age, I always travel with either a *Lonely Planet* or a *Rough Guide*, generally based on which one was most recently published.

I learned that over the past millennium Poland has never stopped scrapping and defending its sovereignty. Thanks to its geopolitical position between east and west, stuck in the middle of two powerful and aggressive nations, Polish history is riddled with wars and uprisings, and the lack of a single naturally defensible border in either direction – like a handy sea or mountain range – made it even more vulnerable to foreign aggressors.

Poland has been the largest country in Europe; it was also erased from the world map between 1796 and 1918. During this time, lyrics were written that eventually became part of the Polish national anthem. 'Jeszcze Polska nie zginęła, poki my żyjemy': 'Poland has not yet perished, as long as WE are alive'. Poland only existed in the hearts and minds of its people for over a century, and it's this immense resilience that allowed it to dust itself off after two world wars, both of which devastated the population.

By the end of the two-hour flight from London to Warsaw, I had the distinct impression that Poland is a nation not to be fucked with. History might be written by the victors, but culture is more often created by the oppressed. Much of the twenty-first century Polish character, cuisine and culture is borne out of the country's lengthy historical tussle with poverty, punctuated with pointed periods of war, darkness and horror. In Poland, I soon discovered, centuries of battered and bruised pride has been distilled into a more enigmatic spirit, a completely winning combination of wry wit, warmth and kindness. Kindness is prized highly in Poland; friendship and generosity never taken for granted. I found Poland's grit utterly compelling, and ultimately charming. From my very first day teaching at that suburban Warsaw school, I was moved by the humour, generosity and sensitivity of the Poles in the face of challenging historical circumstances, to put it mildly. What the Poles had been through, well, it made Northern Ireland's Troubles seem like PMT.

Much of what I learned about Poland I learned from my students at the school where I taught. I accept that this sounds the wrong way around. I trust they also learned a few words from me. I know I lost count of the number of times I was brightly asked what 'gettin' jiggy wit it' meant. But I felt like the winner, in terms of this educational trade-off. Most of my students were around the same age as me, and one of the first things they told me was that when Eastern Europeans tell jokes, the Pole assumes the role of the Irishman. Jolly, well-meaning, but rather luckless and occasionally stupid. Oh! and drunk. But not mean – that's the Englishman/Russian. Or cruel. Or tight-fisted. Those national stereotypes were allocated to neighbouring nations. As an Irishwoman in Poland, I was one of them.

In Poland, I realised that any national cuisine is social history on a plate. Polish cuisine is a melodramatic tale of how plucky Polish cooks battled poverty and starvation with nothing more than three ingredients and a tiny stove. The Sicilians once flung tomatoes at poverty. In coastal Spain, it was fish. The Irish, potatoes. And the Poles, well, they were flinging beetroots, cabbages and handfuls of buckwheat at the bastard.

To the unseasoned eye, Polish food mainly consists of a series of beige blobs and off-beige cabbage, brightened up by the occasional garish flourish of a blood-red sausage or beetroot soup. It's true that sometimes all the colour in a Polish meal is found in the soup. But don't mistake lack of colour for absence of imagination. Polish food is a masterclass in doing a lot with a little. The sheer artistry of concocting a satisfying and nourishing meal for ten with nothing more than a vegetable patch already plundered by some medieval miscreant; well, that takes my breath away more than any showy, visually appealing tiny plate concocted from a series of pricey imported items sold in Wholefoods, and prepared primarily with Instagram in mind.

As an Irish teenager, perhaps I was primed to enjoy Polish food. I'd grown up on stodge. Even now, when someone murmurs, 'Ooh, I don't want anything too *heavy*. That pie might just be too *stodgy* for me', I feel a vast chasm yawn open between us. As any sane person knows, stodge is wonderful. A Caprese salad or a dressed crab has its moments, sure, but sometimes only doughy pie crust, mashed potato with scallions, dense rye bread or pumpkin-stuffed tortellini will do.

My favourite incarnation of Polish stodge was *bigos*, one of those things – like a lot of wonderful things – that sounds all wrong but is actually perfect. Sometimes called 'Hunter's Stew', it's not wildly dissimilar to Irish Stew, aka Everything Stew. But along with finely chopped meat of various kinds and shredded cabbage, there's a sauerkraut kick which I fell hard for.

Today, Polish cuisine retains that spirit of innovation and commitment to satiety, and happily the chefs of Warsaw have a few more ingredients to play with. So there are breezy vegan restaurants like Mango, traditional eating houses like celebrity chef Magda Gessler's Restaurant Polka, as well as excellent Vietnamese, north Indian and sushi restaurants.

Back in 1998, we were still very much on cabbage and potatoes. But the good news was that *bigos*, cabbage and potatoes were phenomenally affordable. Warsaw, with her welcoming and unfussy restaurants, generous 50p pourings of wheat beer marketed as super-posh back home in Britain, and steadfast refusal to let those years of scarcity get the better of life's small pleasures, was the perfect place to be a skint seventeen-year-old from Belfast.

Eastern Europe spoiled me a little bit, for sheer affordability. Ever since, the idea of travelling somewhere that's more expensive than where you live has always seemed to defeat the purpose of travel a little. Of course it's still possible for a Brit to have a thrilling holiday in Denmark, Sweden or Norway – but it's certainly harder to get that whoop-it-up holiday feeling when you wince every time you pay for something. One of the joys of a holiday is that we get to sneak ourselves into a different, often more favourable, local economy, and pretend to be richer, glossier, flashier versions of our humdrum selves back home. It's a thrill to be able to start each meal in Italy with a glass of prosecco, like it ain't no thing. Or order for the table in Thailand without having to make rapid calculations and ask if everyone's okay splashing out on the prawn red curry or if we need to stick to tofu. It's like taking a holiday in wealth. A lifestyle upgrade.

It's why I didn't visit Scandinavia until I was in my thirties. I didn't feel like a lifestyle downgrade, thanks.

My thoroughly-banged-on-about love of adventure travel and job as a travel writer naturally means I'm a big believer in investing in big, life-changing experiences. Trekking in Bhutan, rhino-tracking in Namibia, driving the Dempster Highway to the Arctic Circle – none of these big-hitter trips come cheap, and I'm disgustingly fortunate to be able to dip into the life of a wealthy honeymooner or millionaire playboy and call it my job. Today travel is how I make my money, but it's also how I spend my money. It giveth and it taketh away. Travel is the one thing I'll never feel guilty about spending big on.

But there's a special place in my heart for European cities where a young person on a shoestring budget can still have a brilliant time. Cities like Berlin, Birmingham, Budapest, and some that don't happen to begin with B, like, indeed, Warsaw. Cities that don't immediately make young travellers feel poor, tense, imposters less worthy of a welcome than cash-splashing honeymooners or retirees.

As a teenager, living and working in Poland meant I could afford to live like a grown-up there. All the giddily cosmopolitan rewards of adult life – eating in restaurants, weekend trips away, going to the opera or theatre – were still denied to my generation in the UK, but tantalisingly within our grasp in Poland.

There, my modest wages from teaching were enough to pay my minimal rent to the unbelievably kind Wrobel family who I lodged with, eat out occasionally and plan weekends away. I had no classes to teach on a Friday, so I'd take myself on solo jaunts to contemporary art museums, plugging my head into cassettes that my friend Nikki in Belfast had made me – David Holmes, DJ Food and anything off Ninja Tune – and I'd walk around galleries, first pretending to be interested in all this alien art, and then, in the way that art always gets you, realising one day that I wasn't pretending anymore.

In her own gentle way, Warsaw taught me to be an adult, doing adult things that I could suddenly afford to do. Warsaw was also going to teach me to become a traveller. Although I never found myself lonely in Warsaw – my students became my friends and invited me to hip-hop parties in concrete sky-scrapers and weekends away in the woods – I also plotted a few adventures more further afield with Jo and Laura, two fellow British gap-year students, who were teaching at separate schools just an hour away from me. Because every so often I craved the company of people who weren't having to change their conversation and struggle through English to accommo-date me. I had workable Polish, but I'd also realised, to my immense sadness, that I couldn't be funny or interesting in Polish. I made a very boring Pole. I sounded like the sort of sensible, polite, humourless and unthreatening Polish girl that an overprotective mother would choose to marry her son. But I made a brilliant Irish girl! An Irish girl no mother would wish upon her son!

I'd discovered something similar with French. I made a pretty bland French girl, despite studying French at A level and being in love with French film, French literature and French music, and my near-constant daydreams about one day living in the south of France with a hot French boy lover and being just like *Betty Blue* when she had both eyeballs. I've always wondered if we're different people in different languages. Perhaps finding ourselves means finding the language in which we're most ourselves, most free, best able to express ourselves. Or perhaps it's more interesting to be stuck in the role of interpreting one world through the language of another. At any rate, at this stage in my life I was definitely a funnier and sparkier Irishwoman, and sometimes I wanted to be her for the weekend.

So I was lucky to have the blisteringly good company of Jo and Laura. And one day, Jo and I travelled across Poland in a toilet. We did not mean to cross Poland in a toilet. I'm pretty sure nobody does. We met at Warsaw Central Station, at 6 p.m., having booked the 6.30 overnight train to Prague. Warsaw Central Station is perhaps the ugliest and most sprawling railway station I've ever seen, although Europe is not short of contenders. It's okay for a station to be either ugly or sprawling, but being both is particularly odious. Warszawa Centralna is a high temple to stress and disorganisation, an ostentatious monument dedicated to just how shitty the act of getting from A to B can be. In all our youthful idealism and embarrassing ignorance of Polish customs and traditions, we were banking on this train being nearly empty, so we could sleep on rows of seats all night and arrive, bright-eyed and raring to get drunk, in Prague. But it turns out that Easter is kind of a big deal in Poland, a country with a steadfast reputation – to people more informed than ourselves – as a European bastion of Catholicism. In Poland, Easter is bigger than Christmas. In Poland, to paraphrase John Lennon, the Easter holidays are bigger than Jesus.

The train pulled up at the platform, already so jam-packed

that all we could see when the doors opened was a heaving wall of buttocks, right at eye level. We looked at each other. I figured that where our rucksacks went, we surely had to follow. So I pushed our rucksacks, one by one, between two buttocks. Happily, they were unrelated buttocks, and the bags disappeared. I climbed up the ladder and dived into the wall of buttocks myself, reaching a hand back to pull Jo with me, and finally we surfaced, gasping for breath, in the midst of a grumpy throng in the partition. Poles are wonderfully tolerant about the selfish acts of strangers. None of them exactly exuded a warm welcome to the two new arrivals, but there wasn't a hint of the sort of huffing-and-puffing, haughty British disapproval that we'd come to expect. In Poland, there's a communal under-standing that we all gotta do whatever it takes to get through, and nobody is going to make you feel bad for standing on their toe on a crowded train.

But I was, indeed, standing on someone's toe, and Jo was wedged under an armpit. I spotted a glimmer of space through the crowd, and dragged Jo with me through the bodies. 'This is a LOT better,' I beamed at Jo when we got to the promised land. She looked at me, unsmilingly. 'Go on, sit down!' I said, gener-ously gesturing behind her. She wrangled with her rucksack for a moment then sank down wearily, both rucksacks on her knees.

'This is super,' I reiterated, taking in our new surroundings approvingly.

'This is a TOILET,' said Jo.

'I've got an idea,' I announced, and rummaged in my bag for a bottle of Sputnik, a Polish honey vodka I'd come to love.

Jo began to laugh. 'Just the twelve hours, right?'

Travel makes or breaks all sorts of relationships: familial, sexual, platonic. We were now acutely aware that we'd only spent a few hours together up until this point. But the more we got to know each other, realising that we could entertain each other in a bog for three, then four hours, the better the situation seemed.

I learned a lot about what it meant to be a good traveller that night. Yes, it's important to check train timetables and glance at details of public holidays. But a really good traveller? That's someone who can cheer you up when it all goes to shit. To travel is to invite chaos into your life. And if you're with someone who can't help you laugh when you're facing a twelve-hour journey fighting with your rucksack for space in a bog, well, you didn't pack the right stuff. I came to love and relish solo travel, but travelling with a carefully-chosen friend has so many advantages. Experiences that are shit, tiresome or downright scary on your own can be magically spun into comedy gold, or a charming vignette, if you have the right co-star for this mini-melodrama. As well as having a co-star, and a co-director, you also have an audience. And having an audience, and being accountable to someone, makes all human beings behave a little bit better. We want the camera to love us, baby.

The Sputnik also helped, of course. This was one of those occasions when alcohol really, really came into its own. After six hours, stopping at Wrocław, a few passengers buggered off, and we were finally able to sit on the floor in the corridor. It felt for all the world like we'd just sunk loquaciously into a Chesterfield sofa with cognac and cigars. A little later we got a seat to share. We were now at the Ritz! And, finally, a few hours before we arrived in Prague, we were able to lie down on the seats, and sleep the sweet, deep sleep of laudanum-laced aristocrats at Versailles. As lessons in gratitude go, this was a powerful one. If we'd had those seats from the start, we'd probably have found something to grumble about. As it was, we arrived in Prague feeling like the luckiest girls in the world, our circumstances having made a dramatic odyssey from terrible to terrific.

And Jo and I knew we were on to a good thing with each other. We dumped our stuff at the hostel and wandered the streets of Prague, snacking on rolls, *karotka sok* (carrot juice, which was outrageously exotic to two British girls in 1998, I assure you) and dried fruits, having quite an idyllic day. Our travel compatibility did not diminish. We were both content to exist on juice and rolls, we shared a mutual disregard for museums and we both felt that the best way to appreciate Prague was to wander the streets, rather than reading fact boxes.

We treated ourselves to falafels at the wonderful (and still going strong) Radost FX café, then went to glamorous Tesco to stock up on cheap vodka, Coke, rolls and juice. We sat alone on plastic bags on the steps of the Jan Hus monument, a well-established drinking spot for teenagers. On sunny days, that is. Tonight it was raining, so we had the whole place to ourselves. We felt like aristocrats again, as we had on the train. We got drunk, talked about everything, were witty and flattering to each other – it was like *Before Sunrise* minus the good hair and sexual intrigue.

HOW TO TRAVEL SOLO LIKE A PRO

1. Join a gang

Little bit nervous? Then your first foray into solo travel should be an Exodus (exodus.co.uk) or Intrepid (intrepidtravel.com) group trek, or any active break or course where you're immediately subsumed into a group. Try a surf camp in Portugal or a yoga retreat in Devon.

2. Go budget, not high-end

Don't go five-star. Or at least avoid anything that's likely to draw the honeymoon crowd. As a solo traveller you want a relaxed and friendly vibe; fuss and formality get pretty overbearing when you're on your own.

3. Think urban

A city break alone might seem daunting, but the anonymity and energy of big cities means you never feel self-conscious. New York is particularly welcoming to solo diners, with a long-cherished tradition of bar-dining; Stockholm is super-safe and easily navigable with plenty of art galleries to keep you busy; and in Edinburgh you'll make new friends at the bar.

4. Do your dining homework

Dining alone isn't the awkward episode it used to be. Street-food stalls and farmers' markets make it seem almost natural to be eating alone, and, in restaurants, the trend for shared tables and benches means that nobody notices who is eating with who anyway. Do a little bit of research and you'll never dine alone.

5. Get social

Give crowd-sourcing travel companions through social media a whirl. When I was sent to Austin, Texas, at short notice last year, I found a friend of a friend through Facebook who I offered to take out for a cheapish meal in exchange for their company/local knowledge for the night. So if you're desperate to go somewhere and none of your friends can make it, just book it, and post your plans on Facebook. You'll either be hooked up with a local, or someone might follow your lead and come and join you.

6. Switch off

Try not to rely overly on technology for company. If you can't bear to leave your phone behind, at least stick it on flight mode, so that you can't constantly check it like a nervous tic. A camera or a book is all the company you need, and your trip will be richer for it.

Telling my friend Sarah about my Prague trip in a letter later, I wrote, 'I know that there is a new life waiting for me in every town, village or circus tent. And that all you really need is yourself. It feels good to find my life portable; I can go anywhere and work, sleep, love and be loved.'

Perhaps I've honed this sentiment a little over the years, but I still appreciate my seventeen-year-old bluster. Fifteen years on, I still remember the delights of Prague. The Staropramen, Budvar and Urquell, the maze of cobbled lanes, and the fourteenth-century stone bridges. But much clearer is my memory of the journey. When people say the journey matters more than the destination, they probably don't have a journey like this in mind: the journey of two pissed-up teenagers in a train toilet. But I learned a valuable lesson, a lesson that would shape my travel tastes forever. Travel is all about attitude. And when attitude fails you, there's always alcohol.

2

Scotland: How to Have Adventures

I am firmly of the belief that all university cities should be razed
to the ground and rebuilt in Glasgow's image. With three uni-
versities, the entire city is geared towards students, and, as an
English and politics student at the University of Glasgow around
the turn of the millennium, I felt like I'd stepped into a sort of
student Utopia. Shots of cheap alcohol were a pound, chicken
fajitas at Driftwood were £4.95 and Glaswegians are perhaps
more jovial, and indulgent of youthful high jinks and general
hedonism, than any other urban population on the planet. The
important thing to know about older Glaswegians is this: even
if they exude a general air of disapproval, they don't disapprove
of you any more if you're walking home at 4 a.m. with vomit
in your hair and a traffic cone on your head than if you were
strolling home from work at 6 p.m., saving kittens from burning
trees on your way back from your shift at the children's hospital.
Glasgow is an equal opportunities employer of disapproval. The
other important thing to understand is that Glaswegians mainly

disapprove of things in order to give themselves someone to take the piss out of, or something to tell a funny story about when they get home. Glaswegian grumpiness is the funniest grumpiness on the planet, and their disapproval is all in hot pursuit of banter, which makes it okay by me.

On top of the Glaswegian temperament, the tenement flats of Glasgow's West End, a legacy of the city's heritage as a nineteenth-century industrial powerhouse, permitted impoverished students to live it up in grand, high-ceilinged and be-corniced bedrooms a couple of streets away from the soaring, almost comically melodramatic neo-Gothic spires of the university. A decade later, cooped up in a shared shoebox in Hackney, I'd realise that life had played a cruel joke on me by making my student flat the poshest flat I would ever live in. Even though my mum and I had to scrub congealed vomit from the radiator of my first student bedroom on Sauchiehall Street the day I moved in, this was the high point in my residential life. It was all downhill from there.

In Glasgow I worked at a series of shit pubs and temped as a barmaid at big, boozy events like the World Pipe Band Championships and the Scottish Open. And then I got the perfect job for a skint, perennially hungover student: working at a posh new delicatessen, Heart Buchanan, on Byres Road. I knocked on the door while they were still putting the shelving in, and when the owner, Fi, asked me if I had experience working with food, I said, 'yes'. And then I shut the fuck up. I didn't mention that my food experience began and ended with Abrakebabra. So I got the job, a job I credit with giving me tastes in food and booze that I have never really been able to afford. Essentially, this job – and the one I got after it, at Delizique, Glasgow's other swanky deli – made me posher, yanked me up a few notches on the class scale. Suddenly I was able to talk about Rioja, cook salmon and say 'croissant' without cringing. Apart from one awkward moment when a customer came in asking about 'allspice' and I told them that Superdrug down the road sold all sorts of aftershave, I managed to pass as a posh girl with sophisticated tastes in food and wine. Today, it's pretty much part of my job, passing as a posh girl with sophisticated tastes in food and wine. So I'm forever grateful to Fiona and Mhairi, who took a punt on a chip-shop girl and taught her to like cheese and artichokes and sundried tomatoes and smoky Islay whiskies.

Passing myself off as a posh epicure was all the more remarkable given that I was up late most nights, dancing at illegal techno parties in dodgy, damp railway arches or forcing everyone to do rounds of tequila. This happens to everyone who comes to Glasgow. Years later, interviewing the Scottish actor Gerard Butler for *Red* magazine, I abandoned my questions about the aftershave he was promoting and instead we bonded over just how hard it is to be at university in Glasgow without getting shitfaced every night. The city's hedonistic side is impossible to resist. Glasgow's club scene is the stuff of legend, but also gloriously low-key. The after-parties – thanks partly to all those massive, party-primed student flats – were even better. There was the time we all carried Katie's bed to Kelvingrove Park, so we could join a friend's barbecue without having to get out of bed. The time I got a black taxi out to a rave in a forest in the countryside, and the taxi driver wound up dancing with us until 6 a.m. The time I accidentally went on a date with a gangster, only realising my mistake when every single barman in town gazed at him in abject terror before serving us IMMEDIATELY, grimacing, shaking and refusing to accept any cash. Not that different from being a hotel critic, really.

The problem with Glasgow being such a barnstormingly brilliant university city was that we never had any reason to leave the city limits. My knowledge of Scotland extended from Hillhead underground station to St Enoch, an intrepid 3.3 miles. Despite the lessons I'd learned in Poland, now that I was back in the UK travel once again seemed out of my reach, nudged beyond my meagre budget, requiring a level of commitment I didn't yet possess. (NB I didn't yet possess the commitment to attend an 11 a.m. lecture, as I felt this was too early in the day.) Overcoming Glasgow's powerful spell – *to the pub! right now! you might be missing something! we have fajitas!* – in pursuit of a new adventure took more travel muscle than I then had.

Which was, of course, a terrible shame, because Scotland is one of the most rewarding and varied destinations on the planet. It contains some of the largest remaining expanses of pristine wilderness in Western Europe, a magical place where wild deer roam and golden eagles soar, and midges do their usual bastard flying-into-your-eyeballs thing. In a compact space, Scotland packs a lot in; there are spookily empty white-sand beaches fringing the islands of the Outer Hebrides, the menacing mountainous peaks and tundra plateaus of the Cairngorms, and slate-grey lochs slicing through the relentless green of the woodland like knives.

But I'd explored none of this. Until an Australian moved into my West End flat, that is. Her name was Tess, she was from Adelaide, she was an art student and looked a bit like a young Bettie Page. And she was disgusted by the fact that I'd never seen Loch Lomond, Inverary Castle, Tobermory or Skye. She simply couldn't understand what I'd been doing with myself for the past year.

Antipodeans, of course, are some of the most dedicated travellers in the world. They certainly get an A for effort; many score less highly for attainment. I know Kiwi barmaids in London who pop off to Paris, Tallinn, Dubrovnik and Rome any time they get forty-eight consecutive hours off, hopping on a Ryanair or easyJet flight on a fortnightly basis. It was only years later, when I spent a year and a half living in New Zealand, that I finally understood why.

It's because they're so bloody far from everything. I made one trip from Auckland while I was there, a pricey, six-hour flight to Melbourne. Which, let's face it, wasn't really much of a change of scene from Auckland. If you live in Auckland, and you really crave new surroundings, a different cuisine, a healthy dose of culture shock, your best bet is Bali.

To Australians and New Zealanders, Europe resembles an extravagant buffet brunch after a lifetime eating vegemite on toast. All these wildly varied destinations little more than an hour from each other, there for the taking. A veritable orgy of destinations. Paris and London so close that they can practically kiss! Florence and Rome sitting sluttily on each other's lap! All this debauched proximity is something we Europeans take for granted, and it required an Australian to shake me out of my complacency.

One Friday afternoon Tess casually mentioned that she might rent a car for the weekend and head off to see 'some lochs and castles' tomorrow. Did I want to come? I must have looked at her as if she'd just suggested we go and get pedicures on Venus. A car? A castle? A loch?

Tess deftly shot down every single one of my objections. Between the two of us, renting the car cost little more than a tenner a day. We would sleep in the car if we couldn't find a cheap B&B. The castles and lakes themselves, they came for free. And we didn't need to eat at pricey restaurants; we could load up at Lidl and tuck into car picnics along the way. At the mention of picnics, I was sold. In Northern Ireland, we don't really do picnics. It's too cold, too windy, too damp. Your ham sandwich is liable to be blown away and torn asunder, your Capri-Sun overturned, your Penguin bar brutally bombarded with tiny specks of sand. In Singapore, you had a host of different problems: ants, mosquitos, the humidity. Picnics therefore seemed impossibly quaint to me, conjuring up images of ruddy-faced children straight out of an Enid Blyton story. Even today, my knees go weak at the p-word. I'll do anything for a picnic, me.

Picnics were exotic enough to me; road trips were almost unheard of. Road-tripping in Northern Ireland is entirely possible, but you tend to bump into the sea pretty quickly. From Belfast, most of Ireland isn't more than a couple of hours away, so we struggle to get beyond a 'nice wee drive' and into 'road trip! road trip!' territory on this tiny island. In Singapore, we couldn't drive for more than forty-five minutes across the island without tipping into the sea.

Australians, as befits a nation where it takes over a week to drive from the eastern coast to the west, think nothing of driving for two hours to surf a slightly different beach from the one at the bottom of their road. But this breezy why-the-hell-wouldn't-you? attitude wasn't all that Tess brought to the travel party. She was a brazen castle groupie. Tess knew all about Scotland's hundreds of castles, from the simple, foreboding towers of Hermitage to the moated fortresses of Caerlaverock and hulking clifftop palaces like Stirling Castle. Here in the UK we're pretty complacent about our castles. They no longer evoke images of fair maidens, ripped bodices, spiky torture devices, hurled goblets, malevolent bastard sons, syphilis-riddled warlords and long-suffering horses. To Brits, castles call to mind school trips, under-utilised National Trust car window stickers and the awkward wedding reception of a distant cousin.

So, yet again, Scotland was wasted on me. Most Australians probably knew more about Scottish history than I did, spurred on to a Wikipedia binge after watching *Braveheart*, *Brave* or even *Game of Thrones*. But me? I'd dismissed Scottish history in its entirety as basically the same as Ireland's, but a little less bloodied by the English.

However, Tess's enthusiasm for Scottish history was contagious. Neither I nor a Glaswegian petrol station attendant could shut her down. At the Shell garage just outside Glasgow, she cheerfully asked the teenager at the till if he could 'recommend a few of his favourite castles', which he gamely did, as if every Scot maintains a fully updated mental league table of top-ranked castles.

Perhaps they should, because Scotland has a long history of seducing travellers, and they can expect plenty more inquiries like Tess's over the next few years. Scotland is romanticised liberally, in a way that Kent or Belgium, say, are not. Scotland was one of the world's first ever travel brands and for centuries they've used art, music, literature and the whole cultural gamut to shamelessly self-mythologise. Mountains, lakes, tartan-clad warriors and heroic battles against oppressors – it's a pretty good rep to have, as national reps go. And as a brand-building exercise, you can't ask for more than the novels of Sir Walter Scott, which deftly created an indelible image of Scotland as a land of sublime rugged scenery and heroic chivalry. Scott's novels were hugely popular throughout the nineteenth century, and even though virtually nobody reads Scott anymore (I mean, I studied literature in Scotland for five years and didn't bother) his romanticised representations have lingered in the popular imagination. Centuries after Scott, Scotland is perhaps one of the most fetishised destinations on the planet. Personally, I'm all for infusing travel with romance, wearing rose-tinted glasses as you board every bus, and slathering a thick layer of cine-matic gloss over kitsch B&Bs and gritty city streets. Travel and daydreams have always been closely intertwined, and I see no reason to discourage the union.

I've done my own bit of fluffing for Scotland, of course, writing about Scotland's art scene, banging on about how I'd always rather see a gig at Glasgow's Barrowlands than in any English venue, writing about wild-swimming in Shetland, distilleries in Islay and the food scene in Finnieston. I've even written about my favourite castles.

Years before I became a travel writer, on a family holiday to North Carolina, I mentioned to an ageing vicar that I was considering going to 'college' in Glasgow. He grew misty-eyed. 'Ah, Scotland. It's my dream to one day visit Loch Lomond.' Not quite the 'world's most famous loch' (that accolade belongs to Loch Ness, thanks to a blurry monster photo and a canny PR campaign), Loch Lomond nevertheless occupies a corner in the imaginations of most restless romantics.

I'm sure it never disappoints. The largest freshwater lake in Great Britain, Loch Lomond stretches for twenty-four miles and is thoughtfully decorated with around sixty lush islands. I'm not being slapdash when I write 'around sixty'; there is no precise number, since 'island' definitions vary and some are submerged during high rainfall. And each one has its own unique mini-history. There's the island (Inchmurrin) that was once used as a mental asylum and now boasts a naturist camp and gastropub; the one (Inchconnachan) upon which the gloriously eccentric Lady Arran Colquhoun founded a menagerie in the 1940s and which is still home to a wild wallaby colony; and the one (Fraoch) which autumn visits first, the prematurely russet hues of the woodland somewhat unromantically explained by the isle's poor soil quality. There's not really a single filler, here. They're all good islands.

We topped up our Lidl supplies with swish picnic items bought in a posh deli next to Loch Lomond and I, as a non-driver and therefore designated drinker, sipped single malt whisky along with my smoked trout and oatcakes. Even today, this smoky combination takes me right back to that memorable car picnic by the loch.

Sitting, getting as misty-eyed over the peaty whisky I was drinking as that ageing American vicar had got over the thought of visiting Scotland, I began to see that an adventure isn't purely about distance covered. It's about gazing at your surroundings with fresh eyes. In this case, I had borrowed the widened eyes of a twenty-year-old Australian art student. If you can find a companion to lift the veil of familiarity from your eyes, and help you see life with the awe of a tourist, well, there's no limit to the amount of adventuring you can do. This is one of the major perks of young children. They bring a spirit of adventure into the everyday. Whisky does the same, though, if you can't be arsed having kids.

When I was younger, I was fond of making grand statements like 'the south of England might be pretty, but Scotland is beautiful'. Today I know this is stupidly simplistic, and, like a lot of neat little sayings, patently untrue. But I can still see what I was getting at. The Scottish scenery is gloriously unkempt and a little bit savage; she's a wild-haired, greasy-nosed natural stunner, while the hills of Surrey are freshly manicured and carefully coiffed, with all the easy-on-the-eye quality of a daytime TV presenter.

I realised I could gaze, starry-eyed, at Scotland's curves and angles for hours. She was sometimes so beautiful I wanted to eat her. With my new Australian eyes, Tess and I hurled ourselves into the romance of rural Scotland with all the glee and grade-A gusto that only two giddy twenty-year-old girls can lay claim to. We wandered tipsily around the ruins of Invergarry Castle, wondering which walls had dents from hurled goblets, which of the ramparts looked particularly suited to a spot of bodice-rippage. We talked about our attraction to women, because it has to be said that twenty-year-old women are far superior to twenty-year-old men. Much better groomed, more inventive in their choice of dates, and usually a little less drunk. This was the first time I'd had a serious conversation with another girl who identified herself as bisexual, and we both poured our bleeding little hearts out to each other. Sitting in the ruins of the castle, we wondered if we'd ever find men interesting enough for us to adore. Would it be a man or a woman who'd steal our hearts and rip our bodices? When we were done wandering around ruins baring our souls, we didn't even need to sleep in the car, finding a £30-a-night B&B not far from Invergarry.

And we were home by five o'clock on Sunday night. In less than thirty-six hours, I'd had an adventure. I'd learned to see Scotland like an Australian. I'd had a picnic! And my first road trip. I'd also fallen hook, line and sinker for castles.

This thirty-six-hour adventure was an important lesson, because in recent years the word adventure has come to mean going very far, in as inconvenient manner as possible, and punctuating the whole ordeal with photo opps like eating insects, shooting guns and clinking beer bottles with the long-suffering local sherpas. Today there's a sense that unless you have three months off work, long-haul flights and a motorbike, you aren't having a *real* adventure. This is a phenomenally narrow, decidedly macho and unmistakably elitist definition of an adventure. Not all of us have the funds or the time to cross the Arctic Circle with nothing but our own big-chinned selfies for company.

Adventures can be swift, they can be small and they are most definitely subjective. They can be the tiniest step outside your everyday routine. An adventure is any new undertaking that quickens the pulse. Adventure has a broad definition, and we should fight to keep it so. All true adventure is an inner adventure. It's our emotional response to a change in our physical circumstances. If it's an adventure to you, it's an adventure.

HOW TO HAVE A MICROADVENTURE

Holiday in your hometown. Make a list of museums, galleries or restaurants you've always meant to visit and stick it to your fridge; tick off one a week. Or book a B&B across town and have a sleepover in a completely different neighbourhood. A holiday is a state of mind, not a geographical location, and being a tourist in your own town can be a gloriously spontaneous and stress-free treat.

Jump into the water. For me, the most effective way to slot a mini-adventure into my day is to swim outdoors; be it a lido, a stream or the sea, nothing changes my mindset faster than cold, bracing British water.

Sleep under the stars. I didn't feel like I owned my flat until I'd slept outside in the garden one balmy summer night, wrapped in blankets. Yes, it felt a little bit crazy to be on the ground just a few meters from the comfort of my bed, but it gave me a spring in my step for the entire day afterwards. Admittedly, doing it with red wine and a pretty man made it a lot more joyous.

> **Never plan a dull date.** Whether it's a Tinder date or a catch-up with an old colleague, think outside the bar. Take them ice-skating, blackberry picking, indoor rock-climbing or on a beach walk instead. Bring a hipflask full of whisky, if needs be.

Something happened to me in Scotland, when I began embracing adventure. My heart opened up, and I began having adventures of a completely unexpected kind: dating amazing women. Sitting on a wine-stained carpet one night at my friend Kath's house party, I started talking to a beautiful punk singer named Mia, until, finally, she slipped the hood of her sweatshirt over me and we began kissing in our tiny cotton teepee. I loved looking into her eyes, and seeing her in there. This doesn't always happen; sometimes you don't get a clear view. I learned a lot from Mia, and we shared a love of John Waters films, Pixies songs and stovies, the ultimate Scottish hangover dish. I'd been in love once before, with a teenage boy in Belfast, so I knew I wasn't gay. I also knew, every time I looked at Mia, that I wasn't straight.

To tell the truth, I desperately wanted to be one or the other. At the age of twenty I held pretty strong opinions: about Blur being better than Oasis, about preferring Fitzgerald to Hemingway, about Glasgow being more fun than Edinburgh. Not being able to have a strong opinion about my own sexuality was a particularly cruel joke, and it took me years before I finally made my peace with the label 'bisexual', which was still pretty unpopular in the early 2000s. Being bisexual, rather than gay, like most of Mia's friends, made me nervous about meeting them. But happily this was Glasgow in 2000 and everyone was wasted all the time and enchanted by each other at parties. They all said I smelled lovely and looked like a cat and had the best eyebrows in the world.

During my time at university in Glasgow I went out with two wonderful women; two wonderful adventures. And I came to suspect that women are actually much better at having adventures than men. Adventure has become merged with endurance and survival, when, really, it's something so much more magical than that. It's about the human urge to push ourselves – emotionally, physically, financially, mentally – any old way we can.

And my girlfriends and I began having regular Scottish adventures; hot adventure-on-adventure action. I befriended a gloriously gung-ho medical student called Laura, who married our shared love of late nights at techno clubs to a healthy lust for the outdoors, and the two of us would take off to the Highlands, sleeping in bothies along the way, before coming home in time for Optimo on Sunday night. I discovered I could cycle to Loch Lomond from my front door. I discovered this by accident, mistaking the sign 'Loch Lomond; 7' as a reference to seven miles, when in fact it was twenty-eight miles, along national cycle route number 7.

Even today, I try to plan at least one adventure every weekend – it might be trying out the flying trapeze, dog-sitting for a friend, launching a blog. Anything that quickens the pulse and leaves you feeling human, and therefore open to life and love. Tess, Laura, Mia, Deena, Katie and Kath – these women taught me that adventures belong to everybody.

3

Holland: How Not to Heal a Broken Heart

When I was twenty-one I met the perfect boy, at 4 a.m. in the dregs of a Glasgow house party. Well, he was perfect apart from the Tigger tattoo on his foot, but that could be fixed. Then, after six giddy weeks of techno clubs, 4 p.m. lie-ins and missed lectures, he got a letter offering him a graduate traineeship at a biomedical company in a boring bit of Massachusetts. Before I could even start Googling 'tattoo removal', Luke was gone.

I was heartbroken. And as a sensitive, pallid, Irish literature student, I excelled at being heartbroken. There was no painful thought that I could not sharpen methodically into a dagger; no memory – walking past 'our' pakora shop or bus shelter – that I couldn't slather with extra layers of sentimentality. I discovered a talent for obsession that I never knew I possessed, compulsively hitting 'refresh' on my inbox in case he'd emailed, not-so-subtly asking his old flatmates if they'd heard from him, considering ditching my degree and turning up on his doorstep ready to work as a waitress. Boys love that! They *love* surprise ex-girlfriends! Right?

I'd had the usual teenaged bumps and bruises to my ego, but this was my first time doing heartbreak professionally, and it was awful. Every day without him felt like a pointless day. And I now had a lifetime of pointless, Luke-free days staring me in the face. And the fact that my life was pointless without a boy in it made me feel like feminism had let me down, as if the independence I thought I'd earned over the years was all a lie. I wasn't sure whether I was more heartbroken by Luke or by feminism. A horrible life joke had been played on me: I thought I was a smart, semi-confident young woman with a promising future! WRONG! Turns out I'm just another sucker who needs a man to get by. I hated this new heartbreak talent of mine, and I recall angrily challenging myself to cut down 'thoughts about Luke' from a hundred to thirty a day, as if I was kicking a cigarette habit. 'I know there are plenty more fish in the sea, but where are all the good men?' I sighed, to my flatmate, Wai-Fun.

Finally, I hit on the perfect Easter holiday to get over it: a ten-day bender in Holland with three of his best friends. What a brilliant idea! Who needed therapy or the counsel of wise and loving friends when I could plot such a state-of-the-art emotional rescue package myself?

Obviously, today, schooled by self-help manuals, episodes of *Sex and the City* and *Girls* and dog-eared copies of *Cosmo*, I know that the best way to get over somebody is to sever all contact, distract yourself with a frenetic schedule of new activities, get a dramatic haircut or a tattoo, move in the opposite direction and generally look the other way, pretending you have no idea they're lurking behind you in that sexy tatty T-shirt you totally love. But that's not what heartbroken people feel like doing. We hoard random relics they've left behind in our bedroom, like a Bourne movie cinema ticket stub or an Orbital CD. We friend their friends on Facebook. And so I found myself irresistibly drawn to Luke's friends and former flatmates, because they reminded me of happier times in their grotty communal kitchen, when I was wearing Luke's sweatshirt and trying to find a non-mouldy mug. Cherished, precious memories that I could conjure up when I shared a fag with them, even though I didn't even smoke. Before Luke got his job in Massachusetts, he'd been plotting this trip to Holland with his friends, and now that he was gone from our lives there was a spare rail ticket and a dorm bed in a hostel going spare. For me.

When Luke had plotted this trip with his friends, there was one principal determinant of the destination: the availability of cheap booze and legal drugs in Holland. That was it. There's a travel word association game I often like to shame myself with: say, 'Holland' to me at that time, and my mind would remain a whitewashed vacant chamber, empty save for a vintage bicycle freewheeling past slowly, and a lump of yellow cheese in the corner. There was nothing in my image bank filed under 'Holland'. I had nothing.

I was impressively ignorant of the legacies of Dutch masters such as Rembrandt, Vermeer, Van Gogh, Frans Hals, Hieronymus Bosch, Piet Mondrian and MC Escher. I had no clue whatsoever that modern architecture owes much to the Dutch influence on construction spanning more than a millennia, from Romanesque and Gothic medieval magnum opuses to Dutch Renaissance creations, Golden Age gabled houses, neoclassicism, Berlage and the Amsterdam School, Functionalism, modernism, structuralism, neo-rationalism, postmodernism and neo-modernism – not to mention gutsy experiments in engineering like canals, windmills and other ambitious improvements to urban living.

I knew nothing of the legendary street markets selling rainbows of tulips, sweet herring, caramel-filled *stroopwafels* and cheese. I did know about cafés in Amsterdam, but assumed they'd be little more than a corner Spar for drugs; centuries of café culture, where intellectuals and bohemians would meet up over coffee and cake to debate existentialism and experience the Dutch state of *gezelligheid* (a delicious untranslatable hybrid of conviviality and cosiness), was entirely lost on me.

I was the worst tourist ever. And every time I have returned to Amsterdam since, on work trips to review a slick new city hotel like the Hoxton or to cover the burgeoning co-working scene in Amsterdam-Noord, I wander around faintly apologetically, overcompensating by bingeing on culture and barely sipping a half-pint of beer. I have a lot to prove to Amsterdam, you see.

I suspect that, for many of us, our first trips are prompted less by intense cultural curiosity and more by an intense desire to get pissed on cheap beer or new and exciting spirits, far from the watchful eyes of our parents. But even if it's the cheap wine that lures us on to that easyJet flight with friends we're not even sure we like, while we're in Magaluf, or Amsterdam, or Blackpool, the destination itself seeps into us through the gaps. Gradually we come to realise that a day in Barcelona means more to us than a night in a generic club. We start to think about the local food as more than mere hangover fodder. We gaze longingly at healthy, non-hungover locals going about their fascinatingly exotic daily routines. One day we actually buy a guidebook, and then we are officially travellers, and not just Brits abroad on the razz. My drug buddies and I, well, we were not yet travellers. Culturally clueless, socially irresponsible and entirely skint, we were not exactly the Dutch tourist board's dream clientele.

An easyJet flight later, we were standing on the platform of Amsterdam Centraal when I realised that one of my two holdalls had been nicked. (At this point in my life, I somehow believed that travelling with three, sometimes four smaller bags meant I was travelling lighter than with one large one.) Apart from my sleeping bag, I couldn't remember a single other item that was in that particular bag, so happily the theft was pretty easy to shrug off. My packing technique at the time was sufficiently amateurish and scattergun that I'd regularly glance down at a heavy suitcase or overstuffed rucksack, and decide that if a thief could seriously be arsed carting it off, they were welcome to it. I'd guiltily imagine them waist-deep in a skip, picking through tatty H&M dresses, clumpy shoes and untouched copies of *Ulysses*, before sloping off with nothing but a half-finished bag of Maynards wine gums bound up by a scrunchie.

Thus unencumbered, we boarded the train to Eindhoven. Eindhoven is not high on the hit list of travellers: a relatively drab industrial town that had slid into economic depression when Philips, the electronics giant that was founded here in 1891, shifted to Amsterdam in the 1990s. Today Eindhoven is recovering its technological prowess, with tech start-ups and cultural activity centred around the now-renovated shell of the former Philips plant. As discussed, I have a weakness for such underdog cities, and I fully intend to return to Eindhoven in its regenerated twenty-first-century garb and see if it seduces me. But back in 2001, when we were there, there wasn't really any reason to be.

Well, we had one reason: a friend I'll call Bosco, an affable small-fry drug dealer who'd been forced to leave Glasgow in a hurry for reasons that remained murky, and was now living the dream as a bartender in a gay Irish pub in Eindhoven, called O'Shea's. Everyone in Glasgow was jealous of Bosco's new life, apart from the people who wanted him dead.

THE SEDUCTIVE SIMPLICITY OF SUITCASE LIVING

I'm naturally a maximalist: a lover of stuff, a shameless hoarder of useless but pretty and sentimental things. But in recent years I've forced myself to seriously re-evaluate my relationship with stuff, because I can see that, actually, clutter is the enemy of freedom; an unnecessary source of stress and a sapper of creativity. My guru in the field of decluttering is Vicky Silverthorn, who used to be a celebrity PA (working for Lily Allen, among others) and now runs a bespoke decluttering service. Her book, *Start with Your Sock Drawer*, is my decluttering bible. Vicky and I have had long conversations about why we feel so much more relaxed on holiday, and agree that we shouldn't underestimate the role that simple living plays in our more zen state of mind.

'The feel-good factor of a holiday isn't just about nice meals away, getting a tan, seeing new places,' she says. 'It's also the fact that you have less choice, and having to make a one fiftieth of the decisions that you normally have to make in any given day, well, that's a holiday for your mind.'

As Vicky sees it, we're bombarded with decisions and choice every day, and this takes its toll on us, stress-wise. 'The most important thing we can take away from a holiday is how lovely it is to sleep in a simple, clutter-free room, and how easy it is to get dressed in the morning, because you've only got a handful of items,' she says. 'And how to maintain that summer holiday simplicity in your home.'

If you're looking to declutter at home, edit your wardrobe as you would your suitcase. 'When we pack we look for items that are dual-purpose and versatile, and this is a great principle to take home,' she says. 'The items we wear most on holiday – whether it's a white shirt or a pair of blue jeans or a comfy dress, we prioritise our favourites – this is the mindset to also prioritise in our wardrobe back home.' Most of us only take items we love on holiday, because we want to feel our best, and, really, we shouldn't have anything in our wardrobe that makes us feel crappy, or isn't our colour, doesn't fit anymore or isn't particularly comfortable. Packing a suitcase is a life edit, and we can put this skill to use when we get back home.

Bosco met us at the station and took us to his attic flat, above the pub, which had a pink inflatable armchair in it and little else. The others unfurled their sleeping bags, the flash bastards. I would be sleeping in a heavy satin curtain I'd picked up in the charity shop around the corner. My rationale was this: I could spend money on comfy bedding, OR I could invest that money getting sufficiently comatose that floorboards felt comfy.

If you are an even bigger dreamer than me, and the idea of sleeping wrapped up in a curtain in a Dutch attic sounds faintly bohemian, rustic, quaint or romantic, like something Edie Sedgwick might have done at Warhol's Factory, I urge you to correct this fantasy immediately. Curtains are crap to sleep in. Curtains aren't good for anything other than keeping light out of windows, and many of them aren't even very good at that.

Scouring the room for additional nesting material, I eyed up a spare pillow in the corner of the room, and when Bosco caught my gaze he sprang up and yanked the stuffing out of it. The pillow was in fact about three kilos of marijuana in a massive zip-lock bag, stuffed in a pillowcase. 'When I moved in, the landlord told me just to chuck out the previous tenant's stuff, because he'd buggered off and stopped paying the rent,' Bosco explained. Among a pile of tatty khaki No Fear sweatshirts and black combat trousers, he'd found this. 'Decent housewarming present!' Bosco beamed.

We smoked some of the weed pillow, and went out, dancing in dark, dank techno clubs until dawn, before wandering home, wide-eyed and in deep discussion about what form of cheap carbohydrates to consume. We did this for four nights running.

On the fifth morning, we returned to the attic to find the door ajar, and the unsettling feeling that someone had been in the flat. Then we noticed that the weed pillowcase was gone. Nothing else had been taken; not even my curtain. The previous tenant, the sort of person who not only possesses pillowcases of weed but could misplace one for a few weeks, obviously still had a key. I was a late developer when it came to self-preservation and realism, and it was years before it occurred to me how ugly the scene might have turned if we'd actually slept in our beds that night, as most normal people would have done. Although I like to think I'd have been okay. It's easy to play dead when you're wrapped in a curtain.

After this triumphant cultural weekend in Eindhoven, the plan was to head back to Amsterdam and do exactly the same thing all over again. And on the train, alone in my seat and sober with my thoughts for the first time in days, it struck me that this wasn't quite turning out to be the healing emotional journey I'd envisaged. Obviously, I felt terrible. I mean, I was sleeping in a curtain. And drinking all night and sleeping all day is not a tried-and-trusted recipe for positivity, self-esteem, balance and general wellbeing. As anyone who's not an idiot would expect, I spent all night staring sadly at the space on the dance floor where Luke should surely be, drinking with his friends and wrapping me in a bear hug. Look! There's space for him right there! Why isn't he HERE?

And in the cold clammy mornings I had no one to share my curtain with. No one to send outside for crisps. No one to distract me from how queasy I felt. This was less *Eat, Pray, Love*, more *Smoke, Drink, Snort*. The only thing I could remember from our conversations the day before was a guy called Tristan muttering repeatedly, 'I'm sure something just happened, but I don't know what the fuck it was.' Oh, I also remember Tristan getting very distressed at one point, rubbing his jeans and asking, 'Why am I covered in wax? Why?' Until I looked him in the eye and solemnly swore, 'You're not covered in wax, Tristan, you're not. I promise you, you're not covered in wax.' 'That's really, nice of you to say,' Tristan said, relaxing at last. 'Really, really nice.'

I'd always considered myself a bit of a drugs tourist until now. Me, I was just here for the night, or possibly the weekend: I wasn't a full-time resident in the drugs world. No way. And I wanted to remain a foreigner, an outsider, with one foot elsewhere, alert to the differences between these two worlds. The whole point of smoking weed and taking drugs, for me, has always been to remain self-aware enough to observe that you're acting a little bit differently: being more liberated, saying dumb things. If you overdo it, you lose your concept of normality, and therefore, for a voyeuristic stoner like myself, you miss out on this pleasure of observing what's surreal. I always wanted to be fully aware of the effects of alcohol or substances on me, to feel them changing me, and never go so far that I can't tell how my mind is being altered. It's good to be anchored to reality, even as you float far above it. But could I really consider myself a mere drugs tourist when I'd spent the past five days completely off my face? This was less of a mini-break, and more like moving all my stuff in and claiming my own drawer.

In Eindhoven, I realised that drugs could actually be quite boring. I took drugs to enhance my personality, not to suppress it, but on this trip we were definitely suppressed. We sat, staring out of the window for hours, until someone would say, 'Woah, when did it get so dark?'

Our first night in Amsterdam, we took magic mushrooms and went to see a live sex show, because someone thought it might be funny. Tip: many of the most rubbish things I did in my teens and twenties I did because someone said, 'Come on! It will be funny!' Funniness is not a noble quest. Fun, of course, is. But seeking funniness is the mark of a young, impressionable and fucking stupid mind. At this time in my life I still did things because I thought they might make the teenage boys around me snigger. Trust me, as ambitions go, this is a crap one.

Naturally, watching a live sex show in Amsterdam wasn't remotely funny. To give the thesps their dues, there was a half-assed attempt at a plot: an American GI trod the boards, drumming his fingers to a military chant. Stage left, a women wearing yellow pancake make-up in a racist vision of a Vietnamese/generic pan-Asian hooker sidled onto the stage, rubbed her legs, and said, 'Me so horny!' The GI looked us all square in the eyes (this was easy because there were only six of us in the room), shrugged and crossed the stage, where they went at it, slowly, in a variety of joyless positions.

I think it was at this point, tripping, watching perfunctory paid-for sex and wondering if feminism would ever have me back, that I realised I needed a holiday from my holiday. The next morning I amicably extracted myself from the group (they were all too dazed and confused to object to anything, really – the negotiations went very smoothly) and checked myself into a different dorm in a different hostel, determined to wake up a different person from the girl I'd been for the past five days.

I was faced with a beaming, clear-eyed girl around my own age on the front desk. 'First time in Amsterdam? Any plans?' she said, brightly, as if she regularly welcomed families, business travellers and international jet-setters to the drab dormitory beds upstairs, rather than stoned students fresh off the flight from Luton. 'I thought I might visit, well, the museum,' I mumbled, out of sheer shame. She generously drew me a map to the Rijksmuseum, and, after rolling out my curtain on my bunk and shoving my bag in a locker, I set off for a world-renowned museum I hadn't even realised existed fifteen minutes earlier.

This is the thing about being a British traveller: if someone takes the time to draw you a map to a museum, restaurant or other point of interest, you are contractually obliged, by being British, to accept this mission and return with enthusiastic praise and specific details that prove you were physically there – perhaps even a souvenir mug or thimble, or lock of hair from a waiter, if you're really going for it. The alternative – saying, 'Nah, didn't bother' as you stride past this expectant, well-intentioned local – is simply unthinkable to us. Even now, typing more than a decade later, the idea of forgoing this mission makes me shudder.

And so I found myself at the Rijksmuseum. I even paid to get in! (Paying to enter a museum is also unthinkable to most British travellers, but this felt like the lesser of two unthinkable evils.) The Rijksmuseum is the Netherlands' biggest art haul, with Rembrandts, Vermeers and more than 7,500 other masterpieces being shown off in over 1.5km of galleries.

I'd love to say that I had some sort of epiphany while staring at *The Girl with the Pearl Earring*; that I'm the sort of culturally attuned and sensitive soul who'd ponder the impermanence of all human relations and come to my own form of catharsis via this centuries-old masterpiece. In fact, I was mainly stirred by Vermeer and all the Old Masters' complete disregard for eyelashes. It's like eyelashes didn't even exist in Holland pre-1850. Modern artists, like, um, Walt Disney, knew that sticking eyelashes on Minnie was the easiest way to make her distinguishable from Mickey. Weird. This was the level of my internal cultural commentary, let's be clear.

But even if the nuances of artistic endeavour were lost on me, the experience of visiting the gallery was not. I felt like the sort of traveller that I wanted to be. The sort of girl who'd get up out of her curtain in the morning and head off to galleries on her own. Who would gamely and Britishly respond to tips from locals. Who didn't need to be pissed all the time! For the first time on this trip, I felt brave.

The next morning, I felt like being a bit braver. I wanted to venture beyond the red-light district, have a walk, breathe some fresh air. At the railway station I flicked through the postcards in a souvenir shop, before selecting one I liked: a bucolic windmill scene marked 'Delft', took it to the ticket office and bought myself a day return to Delft.

If I'd bothered to spend £7.99 on a guidebook, I'd have learned that this was a superb choice; the medieval centre of Delft is a popular day-trip destination, and I stepped off the train to find both Dutch and international visitors strolling narrow, canal-lined streets. I'd hurried past the blue-and-white porcelain displays in the Rijksmuseum and therefore didn't recognise it as Delftware, originally duplicated from Chinese porcelain by seventeenth-century Dutch potters. If I'd bought a *Lonely Planet* I would also have learned that the good old Golden Age painter Johannes Vermeer was born here. *View of Delft*, one of his most famous works, is a ravishing idealised vision of the town – Delft sure is given her eyelashes in this painting. But modern-day Delft is no less charming, a thriving university town famed for its architecture faculty, with handsome churches, cute canals and leafy parks.

It was here, surrounded by healthy, industrious Dutch students riding bicycles, that I first began to see a future without Luke in it. I remembered my degree, and felt a flicker of renewed academic fervour, or at least academic sentimentality. Damn, if only I still had my copy of *Ulysses*.

As for these gorgeous Dutch students, well, I couldn't work out if I wanted to be them or kiss them. And I began to imagine exotic, fulfilling romances in the years to come. Why settle for an English boy when I could live happily on a houseboat with a Dutch girl, going to museums, eating cheese and cycling down canals together? Everyone was so glossy, so wholesome, so athletic, and I bet myself that nobody in the vicinity of that windmill had a Tigger tattoo.

In Holland, I had unwittingly chosen the perfect place to mend a broken heart. The Dutch spirit is all about fixing things, improving life and working out how to live a little bit better. The Italians might have the same impulse, but the Dutch have the skills to make it happen. If something doesn't exist, the Dutch can be relied upon to design it, manufacture it, recycle it, hone it, launch it and make it a reality. Today the Netherlands is one of the world's hottest start-up hubs, attracting digital nomads from around the world. There's a glorious sense that anything is possible here, which perhaps comes from centuries of making the seemingly impossible happen. I mean, they even grew eyelashes.

Getting over a heartbreak means replacing one set of daydreams with another, and travel presents us with a vast array of daydreams to choose from. This was my first sense of just how healing travel can be when you get it right. And how travel can simply compound misery if you get it wrong. I had got it very, very wrong ... but getting it wrong taught me how to get it right.

Even though I was the worst tourist of all time, Holland generously handed me a brand new set of daydreams. I returned to Glasgow feeling like my mind had been popped in a spin cycle and returned to my head cleansed, clear and, well, ready to be sullied again by some new emotional upheaval.

Inspired by the students of Delft, I bought a bike, and discovered that a bike is a pretty good replacement for a boy. I bought another copy of *Ulysses* and threw myself with renewed gusto into my degree, determined to get a first, since I was no longer going to drop out of university for a boy and go and work illegally in small-town America as a waitress. I also worked harder at my job in the smart deli, poshing myself up so I didn't let down the Kalamata olives. I got my hair cut like Cameron Diaz's, started wearing make-up again and felt like a supermodel compared to the girl wrapped in that curtain. I began to see that the world was full of possibility, and that the future I'd dreamed of with Luke was a pretty boring one compared to the rest of what the world could offer.

I had been worried that as soon as I slipped back into my old routine in Glasgow my thoughts would slip into their old routine, too. Perhaps I could only move on by moving away. But this didn't happen. Travel *worked*. Yes, I thought more about Luke back in Glasgow than in Delft. But I had been mildly infected by the Dutch spirit of moving on, fixing it up, making things better. And I knew that just an easyJet flight away were a load of sexy students flirting around a windmill.

4

Thailand: How to Be a Backpacker

My first ever real, solo adventure was an accident. I never meant to become a backpacker. When I finished my postgraduate degree in Glasgow I had a different plan. I'd established that I wanted to be a journalist, which to me seemed like the perfect life for a nosy, restless, romantic, secret show-off like myself. I'd also established that in order to become a journalist I needed much more experience than my time at the university paper (the *Glasgow University Guardian*) and a weird, long-defunct local fashion magazine gave me, but I also couldn't afford to take unpaid internships at magazines or newspapers in London.

My plan wasn't particularly sophisticated: fly to New Zealand and wangle a job in journalism by outrageously bigging up the tiny experience I had. Perhaps the *Glasgow University Guardian* could be truncated to the *Guardian*? Words drop off CVs all the time, right? Anyway, I'd work out the minor details later, but I'd somehow maximise my minimal experience, secure a great job in New Zealand as a high-flying, world-travelling reporter, and then eventually swan back to London and get a plum role as a columnist at the Actual *Guardian*.

I had it all worked out. I didn't want a stupid year back-packing around Peru. I didn't have the money for it. I wasn't like those students at Edinburgh University whose parents gave them funds to go off and 'find themselves' atop a mountain in Nepal – providing, of course, that the self they found was an investment banker or specialist in housing law. I only had a few hundred pounds in my account, the remnants of a student loan, and I had fraudulently obtained work to get on with.

It was with reluctance that I agreed to a two-week stopover in Bangkok with my friend Kate, who was also travelling out to New Zealand, to hang out with her cousins. Cousins I could hopefully hit on for any media contacts they might have. Or have sex with. One or the other.

To cut a long cock-up short, we both booked the wrong dates, and we both wound up with separate two-week stopovers in Bangkok, me flying into Bangkok Airport just as she departed. I didn't want two weeks in Thailand on my own. But I had them. My older, wiser and indefatigably worldly friend Laura handed me her battered *Lonely Planet* guide to Thailand and said, glibly, 'Thailand's a piece of piss to travel in. You'll be fine.'

But I was still nervous. And when I'm nervous, I make lists, the way other people bite their nails or smoke. On this occasion, it was playlists on my iPod. Today, typing up these memories, it's hard to imagine myself being terrified of landing alone in a new country, something I've done hundreds of times now. These days I relish the chaos, the confusion and the unfamiliar smells. Stepping off the plane, I inhale the air as a sommelier might sample a wine, attuned and appreciative of its various qualities following hours in a depressingly neutral climate-controlled and air-freshened chamber. I've come to associate this first gulp of unfamiliar air as Step 1 of any new adventure. But in 2004, when I arrived at Bangkok Airport, the unfamiliar scents and sounds threw me, and everyone I saw was a potential murderer-in-waiting. This was not Bangkok's shiny new Suvarnabhumi Airport (which didn't open until 2006), with its spas and swish sarong shops, where rape and death feels like a less immediate proposition. This was Bangkok's older Don Mueang Airport, about to be decommissioned for being too shit, with a run-down, also-about-to-be-decommissioned railway station to match. There was one other man on the platform, and, as every woman knows, one man is worse than fifty on a deserted train platform. At Don Mueang, rape and death felt imminent; it hovered in the air like the mosquitos.

Fear is a fact of life for women, and I always feel my skin prickle when I travel. We might be dressed up in expensive leather footwear and robot-woven garments, and Wi-Fi-ed to the nines, but we're still all cavewomen trying to survive, and there's nothing like solo travel to put us right back in the cave. When we travel, we're acutely aware that our antennae might be slightly off-kilter. We're constantly processing a range of facts about our surroundings, scanning for threats, and when our environment changes, and behavioural norms shift, it throws us. In unfamiliar surroundings, visual clues lose their meaning and our safety gauges fail. On that train platform, I knew that my danger radar could be critically askew. I love travelling solo, but let's face it: even the most spirited, gung-ho adventure traveller has moments when she fears she's about to be raped and murdered.

Every so often I idly wonder what it would be like to be a male traveller. I know that male travellers are not clad in some sort of invincibility cloak, and I know it could be argued that male travellers are more likely to be unfairly caught up in a drunken brawl or mugged. But it must be nice to be spared the raped-and-murdered thought in all its tiresome regularity. It must be nice to go for a run in the backstreets of a new city at 6 a.m. without worrying about imminent violent death, because such thoughts really taint the endorphin rush of a morning jog.

Oh, and men, you should know that these moments of fear are not rarities, or the occasional melodramatic indulgence of an isolated madwomen. (Perhaps I am an isolated madwoman; I have no problem with this label. But I assure you that my fear is entirely sane.) All women have these thoughts all the bloody time, countless times a day. Which is why doing anything at all that even hints at a sexual threat – from catcalls in the street to lecherous stares from your van or sexist jokes in the office – makes a man a douchebag of the highest order. Because we aren't making this shit up: women *are* attacked by strangers on the street, bundled into vehicles, and forced to leave our jobs because of a pervy boss. How we wish we could see those catcalls, stares and jokes as 'compliments' and 'harmless fun', and if all men would just stop harassing, raping and killing women we'd love to join you in a big old laugh about it all. It's only the privileged who are able to deny their privilege, because privilege is invisible to those who have it. We all need to remember that.

So I can't really begrudge my twenty-three-year-old self – a traveller as green as spirulina – my silent hysteria on that train platform, over some poor shiftworker coming off night duty at the airport pharmacy or whatever. At six in the morning, in the cold purple dawn and on a cold, purple concrete train platform, I was fairly sure I'd just sidled up to Bangkok's premier serial killer and in a few short hours my body would be stuffed in my suitcase, my jumpers and jeans and fake-journalist clothes all dumped in a skip. I stood there, cheerfully thinking of headlines the *Daily Mail* would run if I had indeed got off the plane and immediately bumped into Bangkok's answer to Ted Bundy. This was before the days of iPhones, so I couldn't check hashtags for my journey, tweet about my nerves, crowd-source some courage. Instead, I plugged my iPod into my ears and blared the *Kill Bill* soundtrack, which is what women did in 2004 when we wanted to feel like badasses. I hoped that some of Uma Thurman's bravery (and looks, if I'm really honest) could be absorbed through my eardrums. The commuter at the end of the platform turned around and gave me a polite smile, before sipping daintily on a Yakult. I returned his smile sheepishly, acutely aware that I needed to get a lot better at feeling okay about being female, twenty-three and alone in a strange country. I didn't realise what an addictive feeling this was going to be.

Mercifully still alive, I jumped on the train to Chiang Mai when it trundled into the station, and sped north. Rail is a glorious way to travel around Thailand. The trains take their time, smelling every single frangipani blossom they glide past, and rolling slowly through chaotic fruit markets and temple complexes with golden-domed stupas, and giving you plenty of time in each station to buy banana fritters or rice dumplings from street-food vendors through the train windows. It's as if Thailand's trains believe that Thailand is too beautiful to be rushed through, and even though it took me eleven hours to travel the 700km north to reach Chiang Mai, I agreed with the trains.

Chiang Mai, my tentative first taste of Thailand, was delicious. As a destination, Thailand is extravagantly generous with her charms; you could tumble down the steps of the plane and land on your bum in an awe-inspiring *wát* (temple), complex spicy bowl of pad thai in hand and the scent of lemongrass in your nostrils. It's all right there, in Thailand: the colourful patchwork of morning markets, steaming paddy fields, the gilded domes of temples and bamboo houses.

I'd made the decision to skip Bangkok for this surprise two-week stopover because, quite honestly, at this stage big cities still scared me. Chiang Mai to Bangkok felt like Glasgow to London. At twenty-three, London still intimidated me, but a Glasgow-sized city? That I could just about handle. Today, of course, I feel much less wary of capital cities, but I still believe that we get far too fixated on the capitals, when, actually, a smaller city might offer a much better experience for visitors. Edinburgh, for example, is much more enjoyable for backpackers on a budget than London. It's walkable, pints are cheap, the architecture just as grandiose and the people less irate. I'd say the same about Aarhus over Copenhagen, Kraków over Warsaw and Bordeaux over Paris. I love these capitals but depending on your budget, your mood and your time frame, a smaller and more accessible city might get you to the heart of a new destination more swiftly.

Thailand's northern capital is Bangkok's gentle, cultured and more sedate little sister, and, thanks to its status as the former seat of the Lanna kingdom, it's not remotely chippy about its non-capital status. With long, leafy boulevards and mercifully bereft of the traffic-choked urban sprawl of Bangkok, Chiang Mai sits confidently in the rainforested foothills of the mountainous north. A thoroughly modern city has grown up around the ancient historical centre of Chiang Mai, but just a short moped ride takes you deep into the jungle, a place of pounding waterfalls, country villages, eerily tranquil forest *wát* and steaming paddy fields – as well as an array of adventure camps, elephant sanctuaries and crafts markets, all geared up for tourists.

My £5-a-night hostel was in the *soi* (lanes) of the old town, among the thirty-strong temple spires, where barefoot monks, clad in tangerine-hued robes, collected alms in the morning. In the city's medieval prime, virtually everything was constructed from teak wood hauled by patient elephants from the surrounding rainforest. The only notable exceptions to timber construction (which is why they still stand) were the monasteries, towering *wát* built on ancient brick *chedi* (stupas) in a dizzying array of architectural shapes and sizes and styles. What I adored most about Chiang Mai, and what is immediately visible, is the graceful intermingling of old and new. Those last six words make up one of travel writing's great clichés, but in the case of Chiang Mai the cliché taunts you with its inescapable truth. Perhaps more than anywhere else I've visited, Chiang Mai is where the old-meets-new cliché comes out and does a little clog dance right in my face, until I'm forced, belligerently, to nod and acknowledge it.

This ancient capital has a reputation for a live-and-kicking creative scene and a vibrant co-working culture, and is never out of Nomad List's top ten, a ranking system for digital nomads. In Nimmanhaemin Road, the student quarter, it's all glossy and ferociously air-conditioned shopping malls and expensive coffee shops serving flat whites, but Chiang Mai's younger inhabitants haven't turned their backs on older establishments. In Thailand, as in much of Asia, eating out is not about old versus new, as it tends to be in neophiliac European and North American capitals like London and New York. In Thailand, it's about good versus crappy. Old-school coffee shops serving fragrant, northern dishes like *laab* (minced meat with mint and spices) served with fistfuls of sticky glutinous rice, rub up against glossy artisan cocktail bars, and both are equally frequented (and Instagrammed) by locals and visitors alike.

I was in Chiang Mai to do a ten-day Thai massage course, in case my career as a fraudulent journalist in New Zealand didn't pan out. And, really, to give myself a purpose for being there. At this stage I was still an amateur traveller, and wouldn't have known what to do with myself all day. Booking myself onto a course turned out to be a pretty smart move, as a nervous, solo female traveller. I met a cheerful Norwegian couple, Anders and Beate, who were doing the massage course not, like me, as a career Plan B, but because they thought it might be a nice thing for them to do with each other. I was awestruck at such a mutually respectful and adult relationship. I'd never come across such a good couple before. We met at Lek Chaiya Nerve Touch Massage School, a small studio space with pink cotton mats on the floor, where the formidable Mama Lek immediately instructed me to massage the inside of Anders' thighs and buttocks. I can tell you, you definitely leapfrog a few rungs on the friendship ladder when you're massaging someone's arse cheeks. By the end of the week, Anders, Beate and I were virtually family, spending most nights together drinking Chang beer on the cool tiled floor of a bar so new that it still had no name. I felt a bit like Skipper to Barbie and Ken, but I've always had a soft spot for Skipper. I figured she'd eventually grow up to be a lesbian artist living on a houseboat in Seattle, an eccentric godmother to Barbie and Ken's three bratty children.

Massaging arse cheeks by day and consuming Thai green curry and Chang by night, something happened to me. Something that happens to many travellers to Thailand. I realised I was in no way ready to leave. And one Chang-fuelled night with my new friends, I called STA to change my ticket – and my two-week stopover in Chiang Mai turned into a three-month adventure. In less than ten days Thailand had given me a tantalising taste of the life of a long-term backpacker. And, much to my surprise, I liked it. I had nobody to please but myself, a feeling that I'd ever experienced before, as a protective elder sister, a loyal friend to a close cluster of friends, a half-decent girlfriend, a nervily high-achieving, bursary-funded graduate student. It was a thrill to be guided by my mood and tips gleaned from fellow travellers.

But, more to the point, I could actually afford it. I never dreamed that I'd be able to travel for weeks at a time. Eastern Europe was wonderfully affordable compared to the UK, but you were still doing well to get by on less than £40 a day. In Thailand in the mid-2000s, there were £2 dorm bunks, £5 beach shacks, £1 green curries and 50p bottles of Chang. The dying embers of my student loan, just under £1,000, would go a long, long way here.

And so I became an accidental backpacker, and an accidental solo female traveller. I stashed my suitcase full of sweaters and work clothes in the storeroom of a hostel and bought a (probably counterfeit, sorry North Face!) North Face backpack at the night market. After waving Anders and Beate goodbye as they set off for Vietnam, the Thai islands and a few other more expensive jaunts than Skipper couldn't stretch to, I jumped in a minibus to the mountain town of Pai.

Sitting in the backseat with a mix of Thais and *farang* (whities) with my backpack wedged between my knees, being thrown around at every hair-raising turn in the road, I thought about the pale, scared girl lugging a suitcase nervously up and down the train platform at Don Mueang Airport. In two weeks I'd become a totally different person. Once again, I was floored by the power of travel to transform. Thailand pops a lot of travellers' cherries, and she does so gently, with good grace and humour, and makes you breakfast in the morning.

Backpacking around South East Asia is much like a Choose Your Own Adventure book. As well as being affordable, there's a well-trodden tourist route, so I didn't need to think more than two stops ahead. The plot of Anna, the Accidental Backpacker, I decided, was to learn something new in each place. I'd spent the last few years at university in Glasgow getting wrecked and guiltily reading Jane Austen, hoping that her luminous rightness about everything from modern manners to love and literature could right my wrongs from the night before. There had to be more to my personality than booze and books. South East Asia was an affordable place to try the tasting menu (with wine pairings) of prospective hobbies, so I could move on to New Zealand an actual adult, with a respectable cluster of healthy habits and impressive physical feats under my belt, along with my faintly fraudulent CV.

As well as going around South East Asia in search of my personality, I figured that, if I was going to spend a surprise three months in Thailand, I needed to engage much more deeply with my temporary home. So I started teaching myself rudimentary Thai. Even a paltry armoury of fifteen choice phrases massively upgrades your experience as a tourist in Thailand. Being able to say things like 'I feel really lucky to be here' and 'I'm a little bit hungover' and generally joke around in Thai made life so much sweeter, and any negotiations so much smoother. Since very few *farang* made the effort, I stood out. Even today, I rarely let myself land in a new destination without having fifteen phrases in my locker. I genuinely believe that if every traveller could master the following phrases there would be stronger bonds between tourists and the local community. It's a travel habit really, really worth picking up.

THE FIFTEEN PHRASES I ALWAYS LEARN

I have a problem

I am waiting for a friend

I am shy (as a polite alternative to 'fuck off')

You are not shy!

Not enough beer

I am tired

I am hungover

I am happy

Good idea

No, I'm not stupid

Beautiful

It doesn't matter/no worries

This is bad luck

This is good luck!

What is your favourite bar/restaurant/noodle dish?

On the bus to Pai, Project Anna was officially launched. I'd already learned how to massage Norwegian buttocks in Chiang Mai. I was now on my way to do a yoga course in Pai. People are fond of saying that Pai has been ruined by tourism, turned into a mountainous outpost of Bangkok's backpacker hellhole Khao San Road. But travellers wang on about how places have been ruined by other travellers way too often, the same way that people moan about Glastonbury being too commercial and Burning Man a total sellout, when they're both still bloody good fun. Of course I've seen places that have lost some quaintness and charm to intense development over the years. But this sort of travel snobbery – the musical equivalent is sniffily saying you preferred a band's first album before they did that Nokia advert – gets very tiresome. In Pai, while I was meant to be becoming zen and oozing compassion, I started to entertain myself during lengthy *savasana* poses by concocting a bitchy little game of Backpacker Bingo, with a mental list of oft-trotted-out clichés and bogus, third-hand opinions. I began to rebel against the current accepted term 'traveller' and insisted on describing myself as an Irish tourist. Sometimes, finding yourself a identity is best done by finding lots of identities that you really, really don't want.

I even rebelled against the dress code, the standard traveller uniform of cheap cotton 'fisherman trousers' and Chang beer T-shirts from the night market. Having grown up in South East Asia, I knew that most Asian professionals pride themselves on being impeccably well-groomed and smartly attired, and I dread to think what Thai people think of the marauding army of cash-splashing pale-faced tramps that make the bus station look scruffy. My wardrobe of vintage summery dresses worked just fine, thanks.

After Pai, I travelled south, to the rock-climbing epicentre of Railay, a bay of dramatic limestone crags accessible only by boat. I enjoyed my rock-climbing course, but felt faintly mocked by the monkeys scampering up vertical cliff faces while I swung about at the bottom on basic bounders. To enjoy rock-climbing you really need either strength or technique, and after several weeks lifting nothing but bottles of Chang I had neither. I figured I needed another hobby. And it was in Railay that I heard mutterings about Borneo, which essentially sounded to me like Hobby Island. There were seas to snorkel and dive, jungles to explore and South East Asia's highest mountain, Mount Kinabalu, to scale. Plus AirAsia flights from Koh Samui weren't too pricey. I figured that it was worth leaving Thailand for Borneo, because, if I couldn't find myself a hobby there, there really was no hope for me and my personality.

This is how I found myself climbing Mount Kinabalu, having borrowed trainers (just 1.5 sizes too small) from a pleasant Australian backpacker in my hostel in Borneo's backpacking hub, Kota Kinabalu. To complete the look, I had to wear a bright blue balaclava with a pom-pom on the top, which would be traumatic for any woman, but for a Belfast girl it had bold paramilitary overtones, as well as being a fashion abomination.

On the plus side, I climbed Mount K with two Australian sailors who crewed the yacht of a seventy-something-year-old Scottish plastic surgeon based in LA. This surgeon pioneered the procedure of inserting breast implants from the side and now only needs to work for four months of the year, the rest of which these strapping young fellows spend sailing the ocean waves, drinking rum and helping balaclava-clad Belfast girls up mountains. They were such good sailors that they'd even brought a flask of rum up the mountain, and we sipped it at sunset at the summit camp. I felt like I was living in the little-known sixth verse of that 'What shall we do with the drunken sailor' shanty. The fourth member of our little self-assembled climbing collective was an English zookeeper called Dom, with a particular penchant for a rare breed of snail, which had earned him the moniker 'Snail Man' in a *Daily Mail* article way back in 2002. I felt like the boring, vanilla one in our gang, until the next morning, when an unfortunate incident involving my rucksack, a faulty coat hook and a shower conspired to soak my jeans right through so that I was forced to finish the climb in a tiny beach skirt. I'd also now abandoned my too-small trainers for my pink flip flops. In case I haven't set the scene properly, the descent from the summit of Mount Kinabalu involves abseiling down sheer granite rock faces. I was attired perfectly for kicking back on the beach in Kota Kinabalu and ordering mojitos. And I was attired perfectly for horrifying the serious Swiss climbers, complete with poles and crampons, who were behind the sailors and myself. When we made it down to the bottom, we soaked our aching knees in the Poring hot springs, and drank rum, and I smugly noted that, finally, I was appropriately dressed again, while the Swiss climbers looked ridiculous. My favourite/only fashion mantra is one I've cut and pasted into a fashion context from a weed-induced paranoid spiel in *Withnail and I*: 'Even a stopped clock tells the right time twice a day.'

Fresh from the hot springs, I leapt on a bus and travelled inland to Uncle Tan's Wildlife Adventures, a brilliantly rustic (as in, some people arrived, wrinkled their noses and departed) jungle campsite, where gung-ho guides would let us swim in the river before telling us that there were crocodiles in them, laugh about that time a venomous snake fell down someone's top and throw cockroaches at each other. I loved every second of it. I fell in love with the tree frogs, developing a particular love of the harlequin tree frog. I was inching perilously close to being dubbed 'Frog Woman' in the *Daily Mail*.

I'd developed a love of frogs in the jungle and a thirst for rum up Mount Kinabalu, but I wasn't convinced I'd really found my hobby. And so, back in Kota Kinabalu, I booked a PADI diving course. As someone who has periodically experienced panic attacks I was terrified the first time I went under. What if I had a panic attack underwater, a panic attack that meant I got the bends? All I knew about the bends came from the Radiohead album cover, but it did not look pleasant. As soon as I was submerged, however, and breathing into my regulator, I realised that I was fine. In fact, I'd never felt so calm in my life. Diving is enforced meditation, with regular breathing, beautiful surroundings to take in and blissful silence, nothing but the sound of bubbles to interrupt your daydreams.

And, amazingly, I found I was a good diver. I say amazingly because I'm really not good at many physical things. Ever since I was a toddler I've been thoroughly clumsy, and would probably be diagnosed with mild dyspraxia today. My shins and forearms are always bruised and scratched and burned from doing everyday tasks and actions – such as pushing my bike, or walking through a door, or carrying a cup of tea on a saucer *up a set of stairs* – that other people seem to manage without incident. Team sports at school were ninety minutes of ritual humiliation. I love dancing, alone and wildly on dance floors or muddy fields, but anything choreographed or in unison I am shit at. Yet somehow, in a wetsuit, alone, and under the sea, I was graceful, nimble, a natural. A bit like a penguin, really. I had found my hobby.

And when you find a hobby, travel becomes straightforward.

That's the point of hobbies, really. I immediately splurged a seemingly extortionate £120 on a three-day diving trip to Sipidan in Indonesia, one of the world's best dive sites, and, twelve dives later, I was even more convinced that I'd found my thing – my thing that I could do all day, every day, without ever getting bored. Suddenly I understood how other people felt about ski trips, or rock-climbing, or perhaps even a lover.

After Sipidan, I travelled to the next diving hotspot, the Perhentian Islands in Malaysia. My new plan was to work my way north to Bangkok, diving as much as I could, before flying on to New Zealand when my money ran out. And money *was* running out, which is why I found myself agreeing to share a beach shack with a French stranger on Pulau Perhentian. The bored receptionist was in the process of fumbling for the dusty key of the cheapest, crappiest one-bed beach shack when Lio turned up and asked the same question, but in a much sexier French accent than mine: 'Can I look at your cheapest room for a lone loser traveller?' It was shit room, obviously, and after gazing at it in despondency, we looked each other up and down and agreed to combine our funds and stay in a much nicer twin shack instead. I know this sounds insane, but I've always been a pretty good judge of character – plus a sucker for a French accent. When he found out I was a diver, we dived together, and we ended up spending the next four weeks travelling together. Of course, I love frogs and he eats them, which does provoke the odd indignant squeak from me and smug nasal guffaw from him, but other than that we got on great. We managed not to have sex, so we stayed good friends, and are still friends today. He lives in Stockholm and is launching a travel app. I go swimming with his son, Timo, when I visit. So jumping into a bedroom with Lio around thirty seconds after meeting him was a smart decision, after all.

Backpacking taught me that lone travellers are only as lonely as they want to be. If you want solitude, order room service every night, keep your face fixed to your iPad on bus journeys and refuse to smile. Let these facades slip for a second and you will inevitably wind up with a few new Facebook friends by the time you get off the bus. This is doubly so for solo female travellers; when I needed travel advice, help or simply someone to keep an eye on my rucksack while I went for a pee, I could always find a friendly Australian happy to oblige. There's a particularly gorgeous camaraderie among female travellers, a sense that we're all looking out for each other, because we need to keep our ears pricked, more alert to potential dangers than groups of girls or lone male travellers. But one positive, unintended consequence of vulnerability is connection. We ask for help. We form bonds quickly, because we understand the importance of support. Travelling solo, I make a point of smiling at every bus driver so they'll look out for me. I chat to the people I sit next to. I ask for advice from other travellers. Female solo travellers know they are more vulnerable, and that's what makes us better at making connections, and, arguably, better travellers, than men.

Okay, I had some nights backpacking around Thailand when I found myself miserably eating Frito-Lay crisps in bed for dinner, alone in a sagging bed in a grotty hostel, because I'd just arrived in a new town too tired, shy or wary about facing the local night market alone. There was the time I got ill alone and spent three days curled around the toilet bowl, until I summed up the energy and courage to beg the Swedish couple next door to bring me some Dioralyte and Coke. There was one dodgy hostel on Koh Lanta where the owner was so creepy that I couldn't sleep and eventually packed my rucksack and left my room at four in the morning, preferring to wait at the bus shelter with the street-food stallholders rather than in a room that felt unsafe. (After that I started spending a little bit more on hostels.)

Your early twenties are all about self-discovery, but solo travel accelerates the process; and in Thailand my personality rapidly became 3D. I was creating amazing memories, but I was also turning myself into the person I wanted to be, with healthy new habits, thrilling new hobbies, a varied circle of friends, more informed and sophisticated opinions and a hell of a lot more experience. It also consolidated my future plans: I started to rethink my New Zealand plan. Instead, I'd apply for paid jobs at magazines in London, and become a genuine writer rather than pretending to be one. I just needed to find out a way to get a flight home. Because my seemingly bottomless travel fund had finally run dry.

More recently, on my solo jaunts for work, I've been in plush resorts surrounded by honeymooning couples, being repeatedly asked when 'sir' will be arriving at the table, whether 'sir' wants still or sparking water, until I snap, 'There is NO SIR'. And I've found myself in a mountain hut, or atop an NYC skyscraper, thinking, 'This would be really fun/romantic if I was with someone special, instead of a bunch of randoms/this slightly creepy guide.' Being a solo traveller isn't in any way the easiest option, but I learned, in Thailand, that it might just be the most rewarding.

Because I've been travelling solo ever since that trip to Thailand, I've never found the prospect of a lone work trip particularly daunting or dull. And outside of work trips I still go it alone on holidays out of choice, when I know exactly what my body and soul crave, and I selfishly don't want anyone else mucking with a perfect plan. The intrepid British explorer and writer Freya Stark, who died at the age of 100 in 1993, put it perfectly: 'To awaken quite alone in a strange town is one of the most pleasant sensations in the world. You are surrounded by adventure.' Much as I love my friends, it's liberating to know you can hurl yourself into this new adventure right away, rather than waiting for someone else to wake up and decide what they want for breakfast. Travel is the most whimsical of pursuits, and to experience it in its purest form you need the freedom to follow your every whim.

5

Laos: Learning About Luck

Just as my money was running out in Thailand I got an email
from an ex-girlfriend of mine in Laos. We'd met up a couple
of times during my three-month jaunt around South East
Asia, and, in Koh Lanta over New Year, Deena had charged
up the coast on her motorbike to rescue me from a crap hostel
with a creepy owner, and hopping on the back of her motorbike and heading into the Thai sunset felt like freedom, or at
least some sort of cheesy music video. I'm not sure which is
better. Deena was living and working as an English teacher
in Vientiane, the capital of Laos, which borders Thailand,
with a clutch of other expats. The school was short of English
teachers, she said, so there was paid work in Vientiane if I
needed it.

I needed it. But before I settled down into Vientiane life and
the school term, there was a holiday I couldn't miss, Deena said,
persuading me to buy a bus ticket to Luang Prabang, in the
north of Laos. Pi Mai, the week-long New Year festival, started

out as the reasonably sensible affair of spring-cleaning your house, washing Buddha statues in elaborate temple ceremonies and sprinkling a few drops of water over loved ones for good luck. But through the ages, as human beings stopped stooping so much, developed five fingers and became a bunch of violent, crazy bastards, this festival evolved into a water riot similar to footage of Belfast in the mid-seventies, but with brighter coloured guns, big smiles and nipples showing through T-shirts. So not really much like 1970s Belfast at all, but I'm short on metaphors here as I'd never seen anything like it. (And I did idly wonder if we could arrange to convert all the wars in the world into waterwars instead.)

Pi Mai Laos really is one of the most spectacular global festivals I've ever witnessed, up there with Up Helly Aa, the Viking fire festival in Shetland, and Holi in India. There's nothing quite like the sight of pick-up trucks loaded with people of all ages, armed with water pistols and buckets, hurling water at the brave foot soldiers stalking the pavement. We heroically fought back, occasionally even ambushing a vehicle by surrounding it, opening the driver's door and chucking a full bucket of water over him and probably his stereo. And all this is PERMITTED. There are no teachers or parents or politicians there to tell us that it will end in tears or that we'd catch our deaths or that prisons were built for people like us. The teachers and parents and politicians are in the back of a pick-up squirting ambulance drivers in the face. Everyone has a smile on their dripping wet face and the gleeful sadomasochism extends to obliging the soakee to thank the soaker for the faceful of water and the good fortune it brings.

And, golly, it is good to get in touch with your inner psycho-path from time to time. I've always thought of myself as some sort of misplaced flower child of the 1970s, a warm-hearted pacifist who wants us all to live in one big happy commune together. But give me a water gun, and I'm Bruce Willis in *Die Hard*. And screaming while you shoot people *does* make it more fun, so now I understand all those guys in the movies. I found myself twitching if I hadn't shot anyone for thirty seconds, and would simply turn around and shoot one of my friends in the face, then laugh manically and heap scorn on their soggy protestations, muttering 'ha, there are no sides in this war'. From fighting alongside Deena, her lovely girlfriend Maz (who was big-hearted and beautiful enough to not mind me, Deena's ex, crashing their group getaway) and a couple of Irish chicks who pioneered the driver's door ambush, I can tell you that the Celts do indeed make the dirtiest fighters. We tried to get our gang to wear matching red bandanas and call ourselves 'the Water Vipers' but the other nationalities were starting to look scared.

Water is a great leveller: whether it's the sea, a river or a big street water fight, we humans find it good for our souls. I don't think there are enough water fights in the world, and whatever technological innovation and political amateur dramatics we in our developed nations like to boast about, we never invented a happy three-day, nationwide water fight. Perhaps the UK will eventually evolve into Laos, and be civilised, I thought.

But it wasn't just the mass water fight that I loved about Luang Prabang. Sitting at the confluence of the mighty Mekong and Nam Khan rivers, this UNESCO-designated town is simply one of the dreamiest spots in South East Asia, with some thirty-three gilt-topped *wáts*, crumbling Indochine villas and Gallic-infused cuisine. Possibly it's nostalgia for my upbringing in Singapore, or perhaps colonial architecture touches all Europeans with its heady mix of the familiar and the exotic, but I was enchanted by Luang Prabang's heritage buildings and sedate, old-world character. Not far from town there's glorious trekking, waterfalls to leap around in, kayaking trips and river cruises into the even sultrier, denser north. I could have stayed for ever, but Vientiane, and the promise of some cash, beckoned, so I joined Deena and her friends and we travelled south.

A few weeks later, in May 2004, I sent one of my regular group emails out to all my friends and family. It read:

'hey, wanna know what it's like to be squashed by a pick-up truck? i found out, yes i found out. i hope you are all as sick and twisted as me and quite like the disgusting details, because you're going to get them. writing to you helps me a lot, and it's really my way of processing what's happened. but you are my friends and you do unfortunately care and might not appreciate hearing that i bit halfway through my tongue with the force of the impact. so if you are hungover and queasy maybe don't bother reading it. and if you do, please know first of all that i am in a plush private hospital with yummy thai meals and vh1 is playing tears tor fears. my tongue is back to normal, i am the nurses pet and a friend has been staying over almost every night. i am fine. i just can't type capitals, because this requires two working arms, which is more than i have at present.'

Ten days earlier, my friend Sawyer and I were scooting across town on her motorbike after fetching a bottle of vodka for a party that evening when our conversation was interrupted by a silver pick-up truck smashing into the side of us. The driver was fifteen. His father was teaching him to drive and apparently we were the 'stop at red lights' lesson. We had both turned and seen the truck a few seconds before it hit us. It was big, fast, close and even had those metal bars on the front which are illegal in most places because they hurt the people they kill too much. I clearly remember Sawyer glancing to her right, and saying, 'Fuck', which I echoed with a 'Fu-u-uck'. The last thought I thought I was ever going to have was 'not like this'.

I landed face down (with my arms thrown up quickly around my head) on the kerb where I lay thinking I was probably dead until I vaguely decided to respond to Sawyer shouting my name in my ear. She sounded really upset. My eyes were rolling to the back of my head and at this stage things probably looked really bad for me. I'd never heard her sound like that before and it woke me up a bit. I couldn't see anything but I remember trying to push myself off something hard and just flopping back down again. The hard thing was the kerb, and I couldn't manage to lift my face off it because my left collarbone was broken. So, it later transpired, was my right leg (AGAIN, FFS), but it was the substantial head injury to my stupid little helmet-less head that was horrifying Sawyer at this point.

I remember being scooped up awkwardly in someone's arms (a random, kind, important passer-by) and put in the back of a tuk-tuk. I can't explain the unsuitability of this vehicle as an ambulance without sounding like a whiner, so if you don't know just wait until you get to Thailand and the image of our broken bodies on the corrugated iron floor will stop you moaning about the mosquitos. At this stage I still thought I was pretty much dead and was doing this mostly to humour Sawyer. Who was my hero. She was less badly injured than me but probably in just as much pain, and she did just about everything right. She really worked hard at keeping me conscious by making me talk, even though I proved to be quite a pain in the ass as a vocal patient. Very concerned that my jeans had come off a bit and were exposing my (thankfully quite pretty) underwear, I was trying to pull them up over my mangled leg with my mangled arm. Our chat went a little bit like this:

Me: (muttering through the blood in my mouth): My jeeeeans, Sawyer. Help me.

Sawyer: It doesn't matter, Anna. Just stay still.

Me: (scary coma-coming-on silence)

Sawyer: Anna? Talk to me . . .

Me: (wriggling again) But this is a conservative country. Ow . . . help me.

Sawyer: It's fine. Don't move.

Me: (silence)

Sawyer: Anna, please keep talking to me.

Me: My jeeeeans. Everyone can see. Ow . . . my neck.

Sawyer: Stay still. You're hurt.

Me: (silence)

Sawyer: PLEASE keep talking to me, Anna.

Me: (wriggling) My jeeeans . . .

Sawyer: Shut up . . . but keep talking.

Me: My jeeeeans . . .

I don't really remember arriving at Vientiane Hospital, but it was known as a place where hurt people become dead people, or are removed by their family members, who care for them at home until they either become dead people or mended people. But I know that we were put on a more comfortable, or at least flatter, metal surface. In the healthcare section of my *Lonely Planet Guide to Laos*, it reads 'For serious medical attention in Laos, go to Thailand.' In the country of Laos, there was nothing for me.

I recall observing that the only thing making this hospital look like a hospital were the two bleeding patients. It was more like a minimalist stage set in a student production. I don't think anyone gave us painkillers, assessed our injuries or cleaned our wounds. But our friends arrived one by one, looked scared and then smiled weird smiles and started sorting our lives out, which started by calling embassies and getting our passports so we could leave Laos. The strange thing about concussion is that you don't really know you're concussed until someone asks you a specific question and you just don't know the answer. I couldn't remember where I was staying, even though it was Sawyer's house, and therefore didn't know where my passport was. Concussion is like going to a bookshelf to fetch a piece of information you know you have, and finding that particular volume missing. My friend Sarah began cleaning the dust and dirt from my face. She smiled down at me. 'Your hair is all red with blood and full of leaves and mud,' she said, before whispering, 'Between you and me, you look a bit like Ophelia.' I will be forever grateful to her for trying to insert a note of romance, and romance courtesy of my beloved Shakespeare, into this wholly unromantic scene. Deena phoned my mother, and passed the phone over to me. 'Hi, Mummy!' I announced brightly. 'Anna, I know you're at the hospital,' my mum said, levelly. 'What's happened?' 'I've had an accident, but, Mum, it's not as bad as the last time!' I was referring to that accident I'd had in Virginia at the age of nineteen, when I'd broken my femur in five places coming off a bike.

Deena, Sarah, Charley, Maz and Sawyer all looked at me. 'What the HELL happened the last time?' said Sawyer. Because we looked BAD. Sawyer was horribly scraped and her foot was so badly bruised she was in agony. I was a bit more of a drama queen. I was scraped and bruised and bleeding in most places, but the highlights were probably the swelling and bloody left side of my face (I had a square head for a few days), my obviously broken right leg and my twisted, floppy left shoulder. Deena told me later that what upset her most was that my head was on a metal tray so that they could take it away and empty out the blood when it filled up. I was also pretty close to losing consciousness the whole time, so my friends felt there was a real possibility I would slip away, and, due to some sort of sinister swelling or internal rupture, never come back to them. So, in fact, this *was* worse than the last time, by quite a long way.

A man arrived from the embassy and I was with it (or, come to think of it, out of it) enough to notice he looked like Steve Buscemi. He immediately called an ambulance from Thailand, which would take two hours to arrive.

When I'd seen the pick-up truck inches from my right leg, I'd thought, 'We're going to die.' In the tuk-tuk I'd moved on to, 'Am I going to die here?', and as we finally set off in the ambulance,

I remember thinking, 'Okay, Anna, you're not going to die, but the next few hours are really going to suck.' And they did. The two-hour ride to the border was bad, as it was then an unpaved, potholed, famously shit dust road. But I've always believed that two hours of pretty much anything is manageable, apart from anal sex. And so I coped. Although I did rediscover crying at this stage. Charley (our sleepover buddy and general saviour for this first night) and Sawyer tried to keep me talking and Sawyer even invented a song for the road, but even if talking and breathing hadn't hurt because of the smashed collarbone, I really had no good chat at all. I was better at crying, and let my sobs move to the rhythm of the jolting ambulance. It was quite interesting and comforting to be crying so hard, and it kept me conscious.

Everything got better at the border, when we crossed into Thailand and hit tarmac. Blessed tarmac. After the broken-bone-jolting potholes of Laos, we were now floating along, cloudlike, on swathes of silk. When we arrived at Aek Udon International Hospital in Udon Thani, I begged them for painkillers, and finally got my morphine, which immediately made me throw up the iced coffee I'd been drinking from a bag with a straw on the back of Sawyer's bike right before we were hit. The morphine had already kicked in so I didn't care that I'd just greeted everyone by puking up coffee; in fact, it felt like quite a rock'n'roll entrance. Anyway, they X-rayed us and then we must have gone to bed. I don't remember all this. I do remember coming round from surgery to Sawyer and Charley chorusing 'yay'. That was cool.

My collarbone and both bones in my lower leg had been broken and moved around a bit, so they had to operate on both limbs. I now had even more metal inside, and scars on, my body, in addition to the eleven pins that I picked up in my right femur in Virginia.

Covered in bandages, I examined my body with a tiny compact mirror, looking to see if I could find a square-inch patch of normal skin, some part of me that wasn't scrape, bruise or bandage. I couldn't find anything. When you fly off a motorbike into a kerb, every single bit of you gets scraped up and bashed around. I decided then that I would probably never bother getting a tattoo, I would just let life happen to me.

But I felt strangely fortunate. When you hit the ground after being squashed by a truck, and you aren't dead, the only way is up, both literally and figuratively. I found myself in pretty good spirits, although some of this must have been due to the morphine. I definitely felt more lucky than unlucky. That was one big truck. And I'd managed to have my big dramatic accident somewhere that I had friends, rather than on one of my more solitary adventures. Our wonderful friends Charley, Sarah, Deena, Maz and Karen all took time off work to come and stay with Sawyer and me. Some of these amazing women had only known me for two weeks and were lovely enough to do this. It turns out that you also jump up a few levels in friendship when you spend quality time bleeding in front of them; arsemassaging isn't the only way to do this.

And we really did need help for the first few days. In Asian hospitals, as in Africa, the patient's family is expected to play a much bigger role in caring for you, so the nurses smile and dish out drugs, but your relatives (and, in our case, saintly friends) do the trickier stuff like feeding and cleaning you. Happily, a few things about the hospital helped us feel a bit less guilty about dragging people all the way from Vientiane. Our room looked more like a Hyatt hotel suite than a ward, complete with balcony, cable TV and a minibar (or at least a fridge full of crisps and soft drinks). We had room service covered by insurance and – get this – Pizza Hut would deliver to our room. Over on Sawyer's side of the ward it was like a big sleepover with a different companion every night, as they sat and watched *Friends* and ate pizza in air-conditioned comfort. I felt like the stoner flatmate in the corner, out of my tree on morphine, with no appetite and a black eye (it was such a humdinger of a black eye that my entire eyeball was red). I only realised how high I was when I found I couldn't follow the plot of *Friends*, or understand the complex humour. I just laughed, mechanically, when the others did, to try to fit in and look normal.

One day we were visited by a terrified Laotian teenager and his parents. It was the kid who had squashed us. They'd driven all the way from Laos so that he could mumble an apology and his parents could give us small gifts of fruit, good luck charms and sarongs. I could see the horror in his eyes, and I understood that living with the thought that you might have killed two farang girls with your truck wouldn't have made life much fun this past fortnight. My Laotian vocabulary was limited, so all I could say was *'bor pen yang'*, the equivalent of the Thai *'mai pen lai'*, which essentially translates as 'No worries! Take a chill pill! It's cool, bud!' which wasn't exactly what I meant, and probably sounded thoroughly ridiculous coming from my bruised and plaster-clad body and swollen, black-eyed face, but I hope it made him feel a bit better and didn't give him surreal night terrors for the rest of his life.

WHEN LIFE FUCKS YOU UP FAR FROM HOME

I've never been brilliant at admin, but one thing I'll never, ever let slide is travel insurance. Before my road accident in Laos, I had already managed to extract some £150,000 from poor old InsureandGo at the age of eighteen, when I smashed up my femur falling off a bike in Virginia. It was the summer after my first year at university, and I'd signed up to a slightly weird exchange programme where students sell books door-to-door. Seventy people told me to get the fuck off their porch every day. Eight let me show them my books. Five of them bought – and this was all I needed to make a hell of a lot more money than I would working in a kebab shop back home.

But one evening, after getting my final 'fuck off, kid' of the day, I got my bike wheel stuck in a rut on the cycle home and tipped over to the side. It was the sort of fall we've all had heaps of times, but I knew right away this was different. A lovely, nameless woman stopped her car, ran over to help me and called an ambulance. The ambulance guys, while charming, only loaded me into the van after ascertaining that I had travel insurance.

It turned out to be a pretty bad break – my hip was smashed in five places and I needed eleven titanium pins the whole way up my right thigh to piece me back together. Ambulances, surgery, a hospital bed, repatriation and drugs don't come cheap in America, and, two weeks later, when I was stretchered out of

Fairfax General Hospital to be flown home, the tab was over £150,000. Rock'n'roll! I felt like Led Zeppelin checking out of the Chateau Marmont, and I was probably jacked up on similar substances.

£150,000. Perhaps there are some families who could swallow this amount. Not mine. It's no exaggeration to say I would have completely financially ruined my parents, and myself, by springing a £150,000 medical bill on them at the age of nineteen. The recovery process was pretty painful; I was in a wheelchair for a few months, then walking with a Zimmer frame. I went back to university in second year on a Zimmer frame, which is obviously really sexy. But anytime I felt downcast, I imagined how I'd be feeling if my parents were in the process of remortgaging their house right now because I hadn't been insured. And I'd feel pretty bloody lucky. So, trust me: pay for annual rolling top-drawer travel insurance, with all the extreme activities bells and whistles. So that when your luck goes to shit, you still get to feel lucky about something.

Initially I'd hoped to stay and recover in Vientiane, and Charley, Maz, Sawyer, Deena and Sarah all sweetly deliberated over whose house it would be easiest for me to get around in. But then the doctor patiently explained that breaking your collarbone at the same time as breaking your leg makes crutches out of the question, and I was looking at three months in a wheelchair. InsureandGo (sorry, InsureandGo), who were (again) wonderful throughout, told me to come home, where I could have a proper brain scan to check I hadn't become a vegetable. A nurse was on her way from London, they said, and I'd be escorted home on a stretcher and in an air ambulance from London to Belfast.

And, indeed, a wonderful lady called Rosalind turned up, tasked with the job of bringing me home. She was blonde, pearl-wearing and in her fifties, with a posh English accent and dandy little suitcase full of practical medical things. She was the Mary Poppins of the medical repatriation world. Most spectacularly, to me, was the fact that she bustled efficiently. No one in Thailand bustles. They simply glide through life, even in a hospital ward. A lot of the time I admire this slower, more relaxed and graceful way of being, but when it comes to your health you want efficient, British bustle.

The nurses at Aek Udon were all beautiful, polite and gentle, but desperately inefficient. Every time one of them entered the room to take our blood pressure or give us pills, she'd go out again leaving something vital like our call buttons or breakfast far beyond our reach. And none of them seemed to really know what was wrong with us (we had no charts at the end of our beds) so they would regularly try to make me sit up by tugging on my broken arm or pushing my broken leg. I had got kind of used to this, or at least taught myself the Thai for 'painful' 'cannot move, no' and developed a little routine which I performed for anyone who came near me, involving me shaking my head vehemently while pointing at my broken bits, miming 'agonised scream' and staring pleadingly into their eyes, searching for that flicker of recognition.

So, it was a great relief to meet Rosalind and be able to simply tell her what was wrong. Rosalind was a fully trained in-flight nurse who has been lugging broken people of all ages from all places for thirteen years. And she had some great stories about hauling drunken and bruised British asses back from Spain, and an even better one about an old lady who died on her. She had to act normal so she didn't freak the entire plane out. Rosalind also told me (and I believed her, even though I know I am gullible) that Singapore Airlines had launched the longest flight yet by a commercial airline, sixteen hours non-stop. And, having done the sums, they realised this meant that the likelihood of someone dying during the flight was now significant enough for them to build a special storage unit for dead bodies on board. Gross!

For the first two flights I was on a stretcher placed on top of the three aisle seats at the very back of the plane, a few inches under the storage lockers. There was a little curtain I could pull around me if I wanted some privacy or to pretend I was in a coffin. It was all pretty comfortable, except for all the people passing me on the way to the toilet who had a good look at me as if I was some sort of Turner Prize installation. Eventually, inspired by Rosalind's tales, I crossed my arms across my chest and pretended to be a corpse.

Throughout the whole trip I never once saw the inside of an airport. I was simply driven by ambulance to where the plane was parked on the tarmac, and then taken up on a stretcher carried by six Thai firefighters (who all just loved my 'painful bits of me' routine) or by a clever lift contraption. The very best bit of the trip was the Heathrow–Belfast leg. Most airlines save their crap planes for Belfast, so none of them could manage a stretcher or even had a good business-class section, which apparently would have sufficed. So I got to fly in an air ambulance, which was a tiny little plane narrower than the width of a car. I sometimes get quite scared on planes, but this was such a thrill I just smiled the whole way. We flew quite low and it was a beautiful day and the view looked like a tourist board advert. When the co-pilot passed me a copy of the *Sun*'s soaps supplement and asked me if I would like a Mr Kipling almond slice, I knew I was home.

When I arrived in Belfast I was taken straight to Belfast City Hospital, where my poor folks were waiting for their crap daughter. I had put on lip gloss in the ambulance in a desperate attempt to not look too terrible, but there's not really enough lip gloss in the world to distract from a swollen, square head and black eye. I was X-rayed and informed that I had also broken my foot and fractured my skull, but thankfully these had started to heal okay on their own. Again and again I was told how lucky I was. And, weirdly, I felt it. Everything after the moment of impact was marked by good fortune, good friends, good doctors.

But I knew that the hard bit was yet to come. In Thailand, in that Hyatt-esque hospital, high on heroin's little sister, life had been pretty simple. But recovering slowly back at my parents' place in Belfast, at the age of twenty-three, when I'd had such grandiose hopes and dreams for this summer, would be tough. All the doctors and nurses at the City had kept saying, 'Oh, it must be nice for you to be home', but when I was wheeled through the front door of our house in Belfast, to find my bed had been carted downstairs into the makeshift recovery ward of our dining room again, as it had been post-Fairfax General Hospital in 2000, I burst into tears. And then I made a list.

I made a long list of films I knew I wanted to watch, important gaps in my cultural knowledge, as I saw it. I watched *Lady Snowblood*, Kurosawa's *Throne of Blood*, and *Oldboy*, and developed a serious appreciation of violent Asian movies. I watched every single Woody Allen film. Ditto Stanley Kubrick, and David Lynch, although I was never able to get past the bit in *The Elephant Man* when the women are mean to John Merrick without giving up, both on the movie and humanity in general, and giving myself over to despair.

I also made more unrealistic lists. I guess I'd expected to have a bit of a sore and useless leg and arm, but otherwise be in perfect health. So I had all these plans to write a novel, learn to play the guitar, master tricks in my wheelchair and the like. But I was a proper, cartoon invalid for a bit. The painkillers made me feel pretty nauseous so I couldn't eat anything but toast soldiers, I was so sleepy I went to bed every night at eight o'clock, and I rarely moved from my foetal position with a blanket on the sofa. My vision was also quite funny (more like 'shit' to tell the truth) so I couldn't actually read or go online. It turns out this was the painkillers, which was quite a relief, and I hadn't mashed my eyeballs into my head with a kerb or something. So in my first couple of weeks I just watched blurry, violent and vaguely cathartic movies, and my only real achievement was learning how to take off my bra with one hand.

But a few weeks in, I was ready for another Project Anna. I was still sad about some little now-dormant dreams and plans, but I did feel, despite my bruises, one of the luckiest people in the world to have survived something that was obviously life-threatening. When you fracture your skull on a kerb, and acquire compound fractures in two major limbs, survival is a matter of inches, angles, degrees. These had all been on my side, thankfully. My parents were amazing, as they always are, and didn't even get cross that I was scraping all the paint off the skirting boards with my wheelchair. My friends Katie, Wai-Fun, Neil and Evelyn all visited me regularly, and normally found me watching samurai movies or trying to get my one-handed-bra whip-off down to under six seconds.

I had a lot of time to think about what the hell to do with my existence, and began applying, like ten million other hopeful graduates, for entry-level media jobs in London. To be honest this wasn't a bad drill, and I could see the argument for ham-stringing every single graduate for three months and forcing us to sit at our parents' kitchen tables, going through job adverts. The words that spurred me on were spoken by Maz on one of her visits to Aek Udon Hospital, after she'd seen how the vehicles had turned out after the smash. Sawyer's bike was trashed, and the pick-up truck was a write-off, too.

'You two are very, very lucky,' she said, shaking her head in disbelief. 'You both better do something seriously amazing with your lives, since you've still got them.' Sawyer and I looked at each other, and we swore that we would. Then we all settled down to watch *Friends* and eat some pizza.

None of us had any idea how things would turn out. Today, Deena is a child psychologist, working in Bristol, and still the coolest woman I know. Charley works in international development and lives in Brighton. Sarah is a teacher and lives with her wife, also a primary school teacher, in Portland. Sawyer transitioned to a man, which made perfect and absolute sense to all of us, and is now an Emmy-nominated filmmaker and a wonderful father to Devin and husband to Kyra. They live in San Francisco. Maz, our beautiful, brave, big-hearted Maz, died of breast cancer in Glasgow aged thirty-four, after I'd watched her get worse and worse in hospital; ten years before, she'd watched me get better and better. As for me, I got lucky. Very, very lucky.

6

New Orleans: Learning to Be a Reporter

I've always believed in faking it until you make it. In fact, I've come to define confidence as 'the ability to appear confident enough to do what you want to do'. All I need is the confidence to pretend to be confident. I'd never expect the confidence that what I'm doing is right. Nobody has that.

Confidence isn't the same as self-belief. I remember the first time I had serious, surprising self-belief. It was a few months after I was squashed by that truck in Laos, right before my first ever proper job interview, and by 'proper' I mean not for Abrakebabra or bar work. During my months of wheelchair-enforced house arrest in Belfast, flicking hopefully through the *Guardian*'s Media section every week, one job advert stood out. It was a graduate trainee programme, placing five graduates – supposedly the editors of the future! – at five different Emap magazines: *Empire*, *Zoo*, *Closer*, *More* and *FHM*. Today, only *Empire* and *Closer* are still published. In the past ten years, sales of men's magazines, and magazines in general, have slumped like a punctured inflatable unicorn, but back in 2004 I knew that the *FHM* job was the one for me. And, more amazingly, I felt like I was the one for it.

This was the unfamiliar tingle of self-belief. I'd always adored magazines. For an awkward teenager in a drab city, they were windows into a glamorous wider world. A future I desperately wanted. The world of journalism, particularly magazine journalism, is populated with similar misfits. Lonely gay teenagers from Leicester grow up to become rising stars at magazines like *Heat*. Bullied pale emos from Dundee became music critics at the *NME*. That shy, skinny girl at the back of the classroom could go on to be fashion director at *Vogue*. Growing up in Belfast in the late 1990s, I'd fallen in love with lads' mag culture, the writing of Jon Ronson, James Brown, Michael Holden, Grub Smith and Martin Deeson. I loved how irreverent the interviews were, how celebratory of life the overall tone was, how bloody funny every line was, and – at the time – I felt like men's magazines were more positive about women and women's bodies than women's magazines. With a few exceptions, women's magazines patronised their readers with minimal sections on culture, with film reviews confined to rom coms or weepies and the film's calibre dictated by the hotness of some random male actor. Music reviews were all commercial pop, the sort of stuff I, as a lover of grunge and 1970s rock, hated. There were formulaic, sanitised 'ain't she great?' interviews with dull female actors every single issue. I've been a mouthy, ferocious feminist for as long as I can remember, but at twenty-three I genuinely felt I was better served by lads' magazines than women's titles. I also believed that a fearless, feminist voice wouldn't go amiss at *FHM*, *Maxim*, *Arena*, *GQ* or *Loaded*, because every so often these mags misjudged something terribly and made themselves look like a bunch of knobs. I could be the bratty Belfast girl to tell them they were being misogynistic dinosaurs! They would LOVE this, surely.

I sweated over a sample piece of writing, posted over some clippings from the *Glasgow University Guardian* (resisting that urge to truncate it to the *Guardian*) and a couple of weeks later I limped to the phone and reached it just in time to hear that I'd been shortlisted for the *FHM* position.

The job interview was in London the following week. And I still couldn't walk. As anyone who has relearned to walk after months in a wheelchair will know, the sideways, straight-legged walk comes first, which would have been fine if I had been a crab. It's when you try going forwards, and have to start using joints like ankles and knees, that walking becomes tricky. Walking, I learned the hard way, is actually a very complicated operation, with the body rotating slightly along the head-to-foot axis, moving up and down with each step. Tin-man walking sideways, with straight limbs, was much easier. I could do a little Hawaiian hula dance, no problem. But as convention dictates that we humans primarily walk forwards, I was still reliant on both crutches, although I could move quite rapidly, like skiing without the fun. Playing the waiting-to-walk game was getting pretty damn frustrating by this point. I felt like an egg waiting to hatch.

I did not hatch in time for my interview, so I hobbled over to London for the day, on NHS-issue crutches and with all my belongings in a naff little backpack. At job interviews or important meetings since, when I have found myself unnecessarily fussing over which pair of black heels to wear, I remember when my options were entirely limited by my mobility, down to my shoes (practical black New Balance trainers) and dorky little raincoat, one I could slip on with one arm and get my backpack over.

I knew that I'd been shortlisted from about a thousand applicants, and I knew I would be great in this role. And yet! I had zero conviction that I'd actually get the job. A less suitable candidate could absolutely impress them more than me. I was smart, spiky and fiercely determined, but I was also female, and on crutches, and I know to never, ever underestimate my ability to screw something up. You can call it lack of confidence, but I have total, unwavering faith in my ability to cock up. There was every likelihood that this would wind up being no more than an expensive and traumatic compliment that I'd even got this far.

I've since lost track of the number of times I've been told – invariably by able-bodied men – that being female and on crutches must have worked in my favour. Anyone who has ever been in a similar position knows that this is bollocks. The crutches made me feel vulnerable, clumsy and a bit pitiful – all the stuff I HATE to feel and all the stuff we're told we're definitely not meant to feel as we stride boldly into an interview room, metaphorical guns blazing. I limped in, then took five minutes to struggle out of my straitjacket of a coat while my crutches clattered to the floor. (Crutches are ergonomically designed to come crashing to the floor no matter how carefully you prop them up.) And being a woman, let's face it, is a disadvantage at a men's magazine. I couldn't do some of the immersive stunt features, where readers live something ridiculous vicariously through the writer. But I hoped I could bring something else to the party.

Now that I'm a little bit older, I can see my plucky little twenty-three-year-old self the way my brilliant first boss, Mike Peake, did. But I sure didn't feel it that day – I felt like a clumsy little frump from Belfast, an odd fit for the glossy offices of Emap. Even the walk up Neal Street intimidated me, starstruck by this street that I'd giddily read about in the pages of *Just 17*.

It was a good few hours of writing tests, subbing tests and a pop culture multiple-choice quiz, topped off with Myers–Briggs psychological profiling. The night before, in hot subconscious anticipatory dread of all this, I'd dreamed that Derren Brown was on the interview panel, glaring down his nose at me unsmilingly as he pushed a thick line of red ink right through my name on the notepad in front of him.

But I got the job. And I never, ever lost my sense of gratitude, to the point where it spilled over into imposter syndrome. Each morning, travelling up the escalator at Oxford Circus underground, I felt lucky – and convinced that today would be the day Emap realised they'd made a terrible mistake, haul me unceremoniously into a function room and sack me.

I had lots to feel lucky about at this point in my life, not least my wonderful cousin Kathryn, a couple of decades older than me and a million times more sorted and successful, who had similarly fled Northern Ireland as soon as she could, and was now managing director of the London Symphony Orchestra. She'd gamely offered me a bed for my first six months, while

I was on a minimal trainee salary of £12,000, in her flat in Putney. At night, she would be out at concerts, rubbing shoulders with conductors and composers and the royal family, while I'd be at a packed-out Boujis trying not to rub nipples with Jodie Marsh or Kelly Brook.

After just two weeks at the job, I was sent to the Savoy Hotel to ask Stevie Wonder a question at a press conference about his latest album. Being in the Savoy was nerve-wracking enough for me, as was being surrounded by much older male music journalists asking about his use of a drum machine on a few tracks. Because this was *FHM*, my question was a bit different, and I sat there, getting sweaty-palmed. Stevie Wonder is a music hero of mine, and my question, well, nobody wants to ask a music legend and a personal hero of theirs a question mocking their disability. But finally, gently encouraged by another female journalist I'd wound up sitting next to and had confided in, I put up my hand and rose to my feet. 'Mr Wonder, this is Anna Hart from *FHM* magazine. If you ever got your sight back, Mr Wonder, which female celebrity would you be most excited about seeing in the flesh?'

There was a shocked silence – until Stevie burst out laughing in genuine delight. 'Man, there's so many good-looking women out there,' he said, pausing for effect like the smooth maestro he is. 'Just give me my eyes, and I'll go *crazy*.' Over the following years, I came to realise that all the best interviewees are the genuine stars, the old professionals, the ones who can handle journalists and have learned to even enjoy the whole press rigmarole – or at least fake enjoyment with good grace and humour. The real horror-show interviewees are the C-listers, the ones with something to prove, the ones whose names you wouldn't even recognise now if I spilled the beans about our disastrous meetings. I know that just about everything ugly I've ever done in my life, all the stuff I'm truly ashamed of, all stemmed from feeling I had something to prove. That feeling of having something to prove is what turns humans into arseholes. And that's why Hollywood is not short of arseholes. So I'll be forever grateful to Stevie Wonder for being such a gracious and hilarious first interview of mine.

My first year in London was a Year of Yes, when I gratefully said yes to every bananas work assignment, and gratefully accepted every single invitation to every event, launch or party, because I wanted to get to know London, my new city. At the time I was still daft enough to imagine it was remotely possible to visit every single venue in the city, as it was in smaller places like Belfast or Glasgow. In smaller cities, not having been somewhere was sufficient reason to go there. In London, applying this logic is a recipe for total exhaustion and a liver complaint. One Thursday in 2004, continuing to cement my reputation as 'that *FHM* girl who'd go to the opening of an envelope', I went to the Sanderson Hotel for the launch party of a new phone. 'I think it's called the Blueberry or something,' the girls on *FHM*'s fashion desk said, tossing me their unwanted invitation. This was the advent of Blackberry, the world's first smartphone, the piece of gadgetry that would change all our lives forever. I didn't know any of this, of course. I just knew there were free blackberry-flavoured cocktails, and Amy Winehouse performing live in the corner. Afterwards, she sidled up to me at the bar, where I was repeatedly ordering entire trays of free blackberry cocktails and dishing them out to everyone I could. 'They're FREE!' I told her, wide-eyed and delighted. She laughed and I chatted drunkenly for a bit, and she said, 'She is GREAT – I wish everyone at my gigs drank like her' to my new bar buddies for the night. When Amy Winehouse is impressed by your drinking ability, it's probably time to rein it in, but I was a few years away from this realisation.

But my Year of Yes worked, and I soon got to know just about every magazine journalist in London by being pissed and Irish and friendly. I suspect this attitude also helped me swing my first big assignment for *FHM*. At a monthly magazine the biggest challenge is how to cover major news stories when the magazine takes a further six weeks after it goes to press for the story to reach the reader. But when reports of the devastating floods of New Orleans reached us, we knew it was a story we had to cover. My idea was pretty simple, a 'New Orleans: Six Months After Katrina' story, essentially matching up striking images of the flooded city with snaps of how it looked now, interviewing locals and getting some real insight, and hoping to tell the story not just of a natural and humanitarian disaster, but of a socio-political disaster, through these images and quotes.

This was my first ever proper work trip, and I was so nervous about missing my flight that I showed up at Heathrow several hours early, long before the photographer accompanying me, Jim, had even left his flat in Hackney. Jim was a regular *FHM* photographer and we'd worked (and drank) together a lot, normally at ridiculous shoots where we'd be playing snooker with the Kaiser Chiefs, betting on the greyhounds at Walthamstow with Fun Lovin' Criminals, offering shoppers at Berwick Street Market cheese made with elephant milk or duelling with each other on Great Danes. Jim was young and keen like me, a Norfolk lad but also a right east London geezer at heart, and Mike felt he'd look after me. East End boys generally do: they make the best photographers/bodyguards/drinking buddies in the world, and I always know I'm on to a winner when I'm paired with one for a job. Posh photographers are the worst. Mike knew it was a risk, dispatching the junior reporter on such an expensive, important and potentially dangerous trip. He was definitely a bit worried I'd fail, or die. I'm not sure which option worried him more. His parting shot, as I left the office, was, 'Oh, and Anna – don't cock it up, okay?'

As a teenager, when I pictured myself as a successful journalist, it was basically a taller, swishy-haired version of myself, sipping nonchalantly from a takeaway coffee cup with a plastic lid on it – the ultimate signifier of urbane sophistication – and tugging a wheelie suitcase. Inspired, I spent the long wait for Jim at Heathrow awkwardly glugging a Pret coffee through burned lips and yanking my suitcase past Mulberry handbags and stacks of Thierry Mugler's Angel. To be honest, this was quite tricky as I've always been a clumsy fucker. But even though I spilled my coffee and mowed down a few children with my suitcase, it was a great moment in my life, the realisation of this childhood dream. Honestly, I wish I'd had better childhood dreams.

When this trip was greenlit in the office, I asked if I could book our accommodation myself, because I've always been a control freak about travel and I didn't want to be shoved in the big, ubiquitous Hyatt in the city centre. Life is too short to stay in a humdrum hotel, and big corporate chain hotels are really only good for intricate sexual roleplay involving cigars and ripped Reiss suits. As it turned out, my choice of the Sully Mansion Bed & Breakfast on Prytania Street in the French Quarter offered Jim and me so much more than welcome mints.

When we walked in, the chintzy surroundings – all florals and pinks and polished antique furniture – made an incongruous backdrop to the frat party going on in the foreground.

Three twenty-something black guys lounged on the chaise longue, playing video games and passing around red plastic beakers of Coke. The remains of a Popeye's fried chicken take-away bared its guts on the antique polished wood coffee table.

HOTELS: A HOW-TO GUIDE

Don't choose a hotel: prescribe yourself a hotel

Think about what's been lacking in your life lately – rustic simplicity, hipster vibes, sex or glamour – and book the hotel that most delivers what you've been missing. This might mean a slick city hotel, a homely independent B&B, a super-stylish Airbnb in a bohemian part of town, a sexy retro motel or a romantic country house hotel. (Personally, I find cheap retro motels much sexier than country house hotels, which always make me feel nervous and faintly disapproved of, like I'm a slutty and foolish youngest sister in a Jane Austen novel.)

Think about indies versus chain hotels

I used to be a right snob about chain hotels like Hyatts and Hiltons, and it's true that they can be a little bit soulless, and it's always better to support a local, independent, family-run business. That said, budget will always be a major determining factor in my choice of hotel, and sometimes it's worth leaving your snobbery in the lobby and enjoying an affordable, reliable city hotel for what it is. Chain hotels are changing and trying to target the millennial traveller, with affordable rooms, useful perks like a free breakfast, and slick design. And some smaller chains are genuine game-changers – affordable, stylish and brilliantly run. I'm thinking of the Ace, Hoxton Hotels, 25hours, the Pigs, and all the Soho Houses.

Think hard about your 'hood

The way we travel has changed, and we no longer necessarily want to be in the touristy centre of a town, near all the big-hitter sights. These will be easy to travel to, and you'll only want to see them once anyway. What matters more to me is locating myself in a cool and interesting neighbourhood, the sort of area I'd hang out in if I actually lived in that city. So when I visit New York, I stay in Williamsburg, in Rome it's Monti and in Paris it's Canal Saint-Martin. This normally directs you away from pricey chain hotels, too, and into the land of the cool boutique hotel or independent B&B.

The poshest rooms in the hotel, with four-poster beds and heavy antique curtains, were occupied by a smiley dude named Ansel and a couple of his friends, all New Orleans residents who'd been rehomed for the past few months in these plush surroundings by FEMA, the Federal Emergency Management Agency. Every functioning hotel in New Orleans had been turned into temporary digs for residents. Because the tourists sure weren't coming right now.

The guest-house owner, Nancy, had gamely embraced this new era of hospitality, catering for all the young dudes plus two random British journalists, and she brought us empty plastic beakers so we could share their Coke. Ansel, it turned out, was a born-and-bred New Orleanian and a youth pastor (who has only recently left the city to become resident campus minister for student leadership at St John's University in Queens, New York). Ansel was our angel. We pulled out printouts of the pictures we needed to replicate, and Ansel sat there and identified every single location. He even knew where the original news photographer must have been standing to get that particular angle – in one case, up on the hard shoulder of a deserted flyover. And he offered to drive us around town for the next couple of days to help us get the shots, because work had been kind of slow for him since his city sank under water.

And Ansel told me what had happened in August. The warning issued by the National Hurricane Center in Miami at 4.31 a.m. on 28 August read: 'Devastating Damage Expected'. At 10 a.m., the National Weather Service (NWS) field office in New Orleans dispatched a bulletin predicting catastrophic damage to New Orleans and the surrounding region, with the destruction predicted to 'make human suffering incredible by modern standards'. This was when Mayor Ray Nagin ordered a compulsory evacuation of the city of New Orleans; by 1 p.m., the roads were jammed with traffic escaping to Atlanta and the city's airports had all been shut down. By 7 p.m., a crowd of 20,000 had gathered at the Superdome, hoping to be bussed out of the flooded city. An estimated 230,000, around 20 per cent of the city's population, took cover in the attics of their houses. By 31 August, 2005, 80 per cent of New Orleans was flooded, with some parts under fifteen feet of water.

Something that could never come across in the pictures of New Orleans was the stench of decay, and the next morning, when Ansel drove us to the much-photographed Food Circle Store in St Bernard's Parish, the deathly aroma only grew worse. On Day Two of the disaster, the order had been given for rescue workers to ignore dead bodies, the National Guard to ignore looters and for everyone instead to focus on plucking survivors from roofs and attics. Over the next few days, temperatures of 35 degrees brewed sewage, petrol, rats and decaying bodies into a toxic stew. There were still bodies floating in the water outside this store well into the second week of September. Six months on, the smell of New Orleans had matured into a pungent cocktail of thick plaster dust, rotten groceries, mould and oil from the generators being used to power tools gutting the interiors of condemned buildings. During my week in New Orleans, my sense of smell evolved, and by the time I left I was able to distinguish rancid meat from putrid dairy products, mouldy furnishings from rotting timber. On my first morning in the city, I'd simply tried not to retch.

Six months on, a telltale waterline ran from building to building along every street. It was up to our necks on some blocks – which would have been alarming enough, before Ansel told us that the stripe indicated the height the water levelled out at, not the flooding at its worst. Stepping inside the Food Circle Store, the first stop on our sad tour of the city, the smell of rot was overpowering. There were a few people in there with pickaxes, wearing masks. I asked one woman, who introduced herself as Lola, if she was a construction worker. She laughed: 'Honey, *everyone* is a construction worker right now.' Finding themselves jobless, homeless and living off emergency funding, New Orleanians like Lola were willing to pick up tools and help their crippled city out. 'There's no excuse for anyone in New Orleans to be sitting on their ass right now, with so much work to be done,' she said. 'We're happy to help the owner out.' Also mucking in, mucking being particularly apt, was local pastor Mary Scott, who knew Ansel. 'The Food Circle Store is the centre of this community, and it's my grandmother's closest drug store,' said Mary. 'If it doesn't reopen, where's she going to go?'

On the flight out, I had chatted to some fellow passengers who were baffled that I was choosing now to visit New Orleans. Oh, I should have seen it before, they said, when I could have drunk a boozy slushy on Bourbon Street and listened to live jazz in the street. Standing in the sludge in that Food Circle Store, I realised that I was seeing New Orleans at her most vulnerable and raw. I met New Orleans when she was naked and barefaced, not in her tourist-friendly Mardi Gras sequins. And I loved her just as she was.

In fact, New Orleans has always been one of the most open of American cities, a town that wears her complicated, periodically painful history on her sleeve and isn't afraid to talk about it on a first date. The French Quarter was the original

French settlement, founded in 1718, and it measured just twelve blocks by six when it was ceded to the Spanish in 1762, then reclaimed by the French, before being sold by Napoleon to the US as part of the Louisiana Purchase of 1803. That melting pot of European traditions, with the West African and Caribbean influence of slaves and free people of colour stirred in, defines New Orleans culture. Gumbo, the signature dish of Louisiana, is a French-style roux containing Cajun sausage, served with Native American sassafras and West African fried okra – and it's not a bad metaphor for the city herself.

The more intimately I became acquainted with New Orleans, the easier it was to understand why New Orleans was the home-town of jazz, and why writers as varied as Tennessee Williams, Truman Capote, William S. Burroughs and Anne Rice found inspiration here. History had happened to New Orleans, history had happened *hard*, and New Orleanians were adept at using music, the written word, photography and art to process the unthinkable. New Orleans also parties hard; the city holds some two hundred festivals every single year, and it's the one place in the United States where you can booze in the streets and the bars never close. Fair enough; this city has really, really earned a drink or two.

New Orleans already bore history's bruises, and had ridden out tough times with grace and verve. Hurricane evacuations are as much a part of life in Louisiana as hangovers after Mardi Gras. In the days before 2004's Hurricane Ivan, families boarded up their windows to prevent looting, piled into their cars with valuables, toothbrushes and a change of clothing and joined the queues of bumper-to-bumper traffic to get out of the city, when the usual six-hour drive to Houston was taking over sixteen hours. Vehicles ran out of petrol, and desperate families continued on foot. But by late afternoon the next day, says Ansel, the road was under six feet of water, and it stayed that way for a week.

So Katrina wasn't the first, but she was to be the most economically and socially devastating. New Orleans already knew that buildings come and go. New Orleans's spirit – that I glimpsed through Ansel, Lola and Mary – was what the city was built on. New Orleans was gumbo, jazz, guts and grime, not a few fancy buildings downtown. But six months on, a heated debate raged on about which parts of town would be rebuilt and which would be flattened. 'The poorer and the blacker you are, the harder they're going to make for you to come back,' a local resident told me.

We visited the Central Business District (CBD), which, eerily, looked as good as new, rebuilding having been a priority here, as in touristy Bourbon Street. On 29 August, 120mph winds had whipped through the CBD, shattering every one of the 750 north-facing windows of the Hyatt hotel. Nine hundred guests, by then including rescue workers and the families of employees, stayed put to ride out the storm. Charisse Johnson, whose aunt worked at the Hyatt Regency, told me, 'They told us to get out of our rooms and shelter in the corridors. All we could hear was the wind and stuff being smashed up on the other side of the door.' The decision to swallow the estimated damages of $100 million and rebuild the Hyatt was a ballsy move in a city where, six months in, only one in three residents had returned.

But even now, junk still lined the hard shoulder of the state's highways, and signs warned 'Slow: Debris In Road'. Locals became used to the sight of battered boats and makeshift rafts on street corners. One million cubic yards of debris – enough to cover a football field and stand forty-seven storeys high, had already been cleared, but there was so much more work to be done. Some districts, notably the Ninth Ward, were still a wasteland.

Some commentators and politicians had gone as far as to suggest that New Orleans was over, an ex-city, and should be vacated. The US House of Representatives Speaker Dennis Hastert stated, 'It makes no sense to spend billions of dollars to rebuild a city that's seven feet under sea level. It looks like a lot of that place could be bulldozed.'

The Bush family didn't exactly endear themselves to New Orleans residents with their remarks, either. Laura Bush implored, 'I want to encourage anybody who was affected by Hurricane Corina [Corina!] to make sure their children are in school.' Many local schools were submerged; all were closed, but thanks for the tip. Meanwhile, Barbara Bush, Dubya's mum, chimed in with some choice remarks about the evacuees at Houston's Astrodome. 'So many people in the arena are under-privileged anyway, so this is all working out very well for them.' Poor people: they love this shit!

Like any disaster, Katrina created heroes and villains, and New Orleans's own jazz musician Fats Domino, in contrast to the politicians, was a local legend. Ansel cheerily recounted how Fats Domino had refused to leave New Orleans during the disaster. Instead he reinforced his pad with bits of old plasterboard and Sellotape. His home was duly flattened, leading to scores of media reports of his demise. Days later, it turned out he'd been drinking beer on the sofa of local football ace JaMarcus Russell the whole time.

On our final day, Ansel took us to the Ninth Ward and pointed to a lopsided house. 'Friends of mine used to live here,' he says. Ansel had no idea where they lived now, because the phones lost in the chaos cut hundreds of thousands of friendships short.

The Ninth Ward bore the brunt of Hurricane Katrina's destruction. At 8.14 a.m. on 29 August 2005, 120mph winds dashed an abandoned barge into the Industrial Canal levee, which holds back Lake Pontchartrain from the Ninth Ward residential district. The barge smashed over the barrier and came to rest among the houses bordering the canal. Cars, garages and eventually entire houses were swept away as water surged into the streets. In total, the storm surge caused approximately twenty-three breaches in drainage canal and navigational canal levees and floodwalls, and the failure of structures is considered by experts to be the worst engineering disaster in the history of the United States.

Where Ansel had taken us was the lucky end of the street; five blocks away, he told us, people could drive down a bulldozed street searching for their home, and find nothing but a pile of rubble. As they sifted through the debris, they realised they were not even looking at their own possessions. The Chevy wrapped around the tree in the garden wasn't their car. The wedding photos, the leather jacket and the smashed Guns N' Roses CDs could have belonged to anyone within a five-mile radius.

With the nearest open shop now a twenty-five-minute drive

away, Red Cross vans were still distributing food to anyone in the area. We stopped and spoke to Marie Boucharie, a local teacher, who told me, 'The worst thing about returning to New Orleans was the stench. As soon as you got over the state border, you could smell it. While we were away, our city had literally rotted.'

We drove through the silent streets, and in the entire quarter we found only one man trying to rebuild his house. My eyes could hardly take it all in: cars in trees, houses on top of the trailers that once sat in the driveway, uprooted trees splayed sideways across cul-de-sacs. Powerless cables were still draped over mouldering cars, and even the stray dogs that used to howl in these streets had now starved or been taken to the pound. And littered everywhere were tiny relics of normality: small items of jewellery or children's toys, their triviality only serving to heighten the immense tragedy of this decimated community. Everything looked hopelessly, distressingly wrong. The mark of any true disaster – be it natural or political – is that it steps into surreal territory.

'This place used to have such a buzz,' sighed Ansel. 'Today it's a ghost town.'

Over the course of my career since reporting on New Orleans, writing for the *Guardian, Grazia, Stylist*, the *Daily Telegraph, Total Politics* and *The Times*, the assignments I've been most excited about have always straddled several sections of any newspaper: a bit of travel, a sliver of culture, a chunk of politics and a whole lot of social interest. This was the first assignment I could really get my teeth into, and I knew I was only scraping the surface of what had happened to New Orleans.

Naturally, I have a thoroughly Irish reluctance to trouble anyone, and, deep down, I'm shy and awkward. But every morning in New Orleans I looked into my chintzy gilt-framed mirror, feeling a bit like Blanche Dubois but obviously much less soft and simpering, and murmured this mantra: 'You can go and talk to everyone, because it is your fucking job and you are a travelling badass.'

And, much to my relief, nobody in New Orleans was shy about talking to a rookie reporter like me. Everybody had an opinion and a story to tell. And they *wanted* to talk to me. Many felt their voices were missing from all the column inches and Fox News reports about the disaster. The official death toll, according to the Louisiana Department of Health, was 1,464. This number was disproportionately made up of elderly people living near levee breaches in the Lower Ninth Ward and Lakeview neighbourhoods of New Orleans, and people who, for socio-economic reasons, didn't have access to TV and therefore weren't reached by news reports and evacuation notices. On top of being a natural and an engineering disaster, Katrina was also an urban planning disaster, a socio-political disaster and a humanitarian disaster.

There was so much to probe, to investigate, to explore. And I started to realise that perhaps I wasn't an imposter. Perhaps I really was that grown-up reporter version of myself, although admittedly without the swishy hair and still unable to carry a takeaway coffee without spilling it on my shoes.

Because it turned out that I *was* good at talking to people. (My Year of Yes, and being Irish and drunk at every party in London, had made me bloody good at it.) I had a keen eye for the absurd and the darkly humorous, which meant I saw stories that the major news outlets skipped. A friendly construction worker called Jake showed me a tiny booklet that was doing the rounds of New Orleans, titled 'Katrina Fridges', a compendium of sumptuous images of the stylish interiors of abandoned fridges. Katrina's fridges were the stuff of legend – and the stuff of nightmares. 'When you enter a new home, the first thing you wanna do is get a load of gaffer tape and wrap it around the fridge,' he advised. 'If you screw up and tip it over, you're going to be real unpopular. Because that house is going to STINK. Rancid, wet pork that's been stewing for six months? It doesn't get grosser.'

Gradually, my panic subsided: I had not cocked this assignment up. Mike would be proud of me. And I was grateful to New Orleans for being such a generous, open, raw and gutsy city. Stevie Wonder had been my first celebrity interview, and New Orleans my first press trip; two old professionals who didn't hold back.

And now I had the honour of telling New Orleans's story, of processing it in my own small way. Being a writer means travelling with purpose, having a reason to be anywhere and everywhere. I can't imagine travelling without writing, or writing without travelling; to me the two go together like salt and vinegar on chips. There was nowhere better than New Orleans to come and learn to be bold, to go forth and be nosy, to do my job. To find stories, and find a way to tell them. New Orleans taught me that, for me, travel writing would never be about hotel reviews; it would be about politics, people and culture. Stories that need to be told, waiting for me, all over the world.

7

New Zealand: Kicking the City Habit

During my teens and twenties I was a city girl through and through. I know people who feel smothered by cities. I felt smothered by the countryside. The lack of buzz, the lack of culture, the lack of people, the lack of mobility, the lack of diversity, the lack of soya milk; I saw the countryside as a collection of voids. I saw nature in terms of what it lacked, which was civilisation.

I was capable of appreciating dramatic landscapes. I quite enjoyed a walk. But after a few years living in Hackney, I knew I'd much rather have strolled London's South Bank, a fizzing cultural cacophony, than a dull towpath in Surrey. I never felt oppressed by the city, quite the opposite. I felt invigorated by London's career-driven momentum, galvanised by the music scene in Glasgow, star-struck by the swagger of New York, seduced by the rhythm of Austin, thrilled by Detroit's optimism, dazzled by Naples' chaotic charm and moved by Singapore's eagerness to please. Cities and I, we understood each other. And large cities have more in common with other large cities across the world than they do with the countryside or suburban drear that surrounds them. When you've loved one large city, it's easy to love another. You already have the road map, and will come to love this new city, through coffee shops, riverside walks, food trucks, vintage stores, tiny alleyways, architecture and art.

Cities had my heart. Sean, my new boyfriend, felt differently. He grew up on a croft in Shetland. He'd turned turf. I hadn't even burned turf. Sean could tell the difference between neeps and tatties from the green bit sticking out of the soil, when I didn't even know that there was any greenery attached to potatoes, and it was a good few Burns Nights before I worked out that a neep was a turnip. (I'd had the same problem with Spurs and Tottenham Hotspur, though; for someone who makes a living out of words, I can be remarkably obtuse.)

But Sean had moved from Glasgow to London to be with me, without bleating about it or turning it into some sort of power struggle or romantic melodrama. This made him my hero. Sean was the first man I'd met who treated my job, my friends, my needs and my feelings as 100 per cent equal to his own. He didn't care that my job at *FHM* obviously meant more to me than his job – as a sound engineer – did to him. He didn't care that he did more of the housework. He didn't care that I earned more. He didn't care that I made most of our social plans, booked all our trips, and generally presented him with an itinerary every week. None of this showed up as a blip on his radar as an issue. I was amazed. It's not possible to emasculate a man who hasn't built his sense of self on macho principles. This meant I found him sexier, stronger, braver and more of a man than any other male I'd ever met.

But there's something I need to tell you about Sean. He doesn't really like travelling. I still remember him dropping this bombshell, as we left the pub having waved goodbye to our friends Jenny and Dave, who were heading off on a one-year round-the-world overland trip. 'Wouldn't you love to do this one day?' I'd asked Sean, dreamily. And there was a silence. I looked at him. 'Wouldn't you?' I demanded, threateningly. 'Um, to be honest I've never really had the urge,' Sean said. As if it was NO BIG DEAL. To me, this was like saying you didn't really like food, you'd happily just pop a calorie-and-vitamin pill rather than bother with an actual meal. Or having no favourite bands because you 'don't really care about music'. How could he not want to travel? Did he even have a pulse?

At this stage I was working as a writer and commissioning editor on the features desk at *Grazia*, a job that involved a lot of twelve-hour days in our Covent Garden office and a great deal of travel. I was sent to Abu Dhabi, to stay in the world's most expensive hotel, complete with gold taps in the bathrooms and gifts of diamonds and guns for guests. I covered festivals like Glastonbury, Port Eliot and Sonar. I tried out high-end dating apps in New York and tried to bag myself a celebrity. I joined anti-capitalism rallies at the Stock Exchange in London and Wall Street in New York, I went to twerkshops and I covered the Amanda Knox trial in Perugia. My job at *Grazia* was a deliciously varied diet, veering schizophrenically between highbrow and lowbrow culture, hard-hitting news and celebrity interviews, and days of impossible glamour – champagne tastings at Claridge's – with days of relentless grit and gloom, lurking outside the High Courts and following high-profile murder trials.

Because travel had started to become part of my job, I wasn't too worried that my boyfriend didn't want to travel with me. My job would take me all around the world, like James Bond or a millionaire playboy, before depositing me back in Dalston and into Sean's waiting arms. Perhaps this would be the best of both worlds.

Even though things had been going well with Sean for a while, I was completely floored when he proposed. I'd just been getting used to being a girlfriend, frankly, and a girlfriend to a *boy*, when all of a sudden I became a fi-an-cée. At our friend Simon's thirtieth birthday in Cornwall, Sean asked me to step outside with him, in a low, urgent voice that sounded entirely wrong at a ridiculous fancy-dress party. I was dressed as Saturn, complete with hula hoops around my waist suspended by clear fishing line. Sean was dressed as Sherlock Holmes. My initial thought was 'Babe, it's way too early to be puking.'

We went outside, he sat me on a rock and got down on one knee – and that's when it hit me. HOLY SHIT HE'S GOING TO PROPOSE. (Side note: I think this is why the bended knee thing is a tradition worth keeping, even as marriage finally evolves to include same-sex marriages, female proposals, whatever. Just so drunken lovers can actually work out what's going on when they're being proposed to.)

I didn't really think about whether I wanted to be married. My yes was to loving Sean, more than I'd loved anyone before him. While this was the perfect proposal for me – drunk and spontaneous and at a party, how romantic, like something Dylan Thomas or Zelda Fitzgerald would do – I probably should have given this more thought. Because we spent the next two years bickering about my unwillingness to actually get hitched.

I guess there are brides-to-be who dream about their wedding dress, and brides-to-be who dream about their honeymoon. As you'd guess, I'm a flag-waving, trumpet-tooting member of the latter camp. I had a lot of fun daydreaming about lengthy honeymoons – perhaps backpacking around Bolivia? Diving in Borneo? Trekking in Bhutan? Once, again, I was also willing to consider destinations that did not begin with the letter B.

But as soon as Sean mentioned the actual wedding, I panicked. Because weddings are crazy things. Working 8 a.m.–8 p.m. shifts with boozy nights virtually every day of the week, there really didn't seem like a good time to hit the pause button on my life to organise a mini-Glastonbury. There was also the matter of the non-existent savings: all our cash went on the rent of our Dalston flat, with a little bit left over for falafels, porridge and Rioja. But if I'm honest, and I guess in your own book you should be, the thought of placing myself centre stage and inviting a flood of fuss, frills and faff horrified me. The idea of being the centre of attention in a stupid white dress while I stressed out about idiotic shit like seating plans and vegetarian options – this seemed to me the very antithesis of the best day of my life. I'm awkward and self-conscious at the best of times. I chose to graduate *in absentia* from Glasgow University because even that sounded too pompous and stressful. My own wedding day? This seemed like graduation on steroids, or a hefty dose of LSD.

Finally, my eminently wise friend Katharine effectively staged an intervention, sat us down and asked us to whittle down what we actually wanted from a wedding. My main aims were thus:

To finish the day married to Sean, without fighting with Sean, or my mum.

To have a vaguely romantic day with Sean.

To dance with all our mates in celebration of our love, because love is definitely worth celebrating – whether you do it with a wedding or not, that's up to you.

Sean was in agreement, but also wanted nothing to do with a church whatsoever, having been thoroughly burned by an uber-religious upbringing in Shetland. He also wanted it to be sufficiently big that the weirdness of his mum turning up with a fairly new husband would be diluted.

As a threesome, we hit upon a plan. And, two months later, Sean and I got hitched in a registry office in Bath, which we'd chosen because we once had a bloody lovely weekend there, and I'm a Jane Austen nut and therefore find anything in Bath unreservedly romantic. We stayed the night at the Priory, the posh country house hotel that we'd dined at our very first weekend away in Bath, when we both daydreamed about staying there 'one day'. The next morning we lazed in the rooftop spa pools of Bath Spa, then easyJetted it up to Glasgow for a piss-up and ceilidh above an old pub.

It was a pretty perfect wedding weekend for me, minimising fuss and faff, but maximising fun and friends. Naturally, this whole low-key plan would have disintegrated had any one of our five parents started weeping down the phone, but they were all brilliant. With their trademark kindness, my parents professed to be chuffed that I'd given serious thought to what mattered in a wedding, shunned the commercial crap, and, mainly, that I was marrying a man they didn't think was a total dickhead.

And it worked. I have deliriously happy memories of my super-swish wedding. When the wedding party totals two, you can totally afford a Michelin-starred meal! We felt posh for the day, which is really the point of a wedding, and increasingly hard for normal young people to achieve. I even felt posh in my vintage-inspired white broderie anglaise dress that actually cost just £39 from M&S. This saving meant I could spend heaps on lingerie from Agent Provocateur, and deliver myself to Sean with the words, 'Your wife's a slut'. I was still wearing the dress on Sunday night (with a few washes in between, me and the dress) at Optimo, my favourite club, until we finally called time on our wedding celebrations at 3 a.m.

I'd love to tell you that we then strapped on our rucksacks, mine over a grubby and wine-stained wedding dress, and jetted off then and there. Instead, we went back to sleep on an air mattress in my old student flat in Glasgow's West End, and started stripping wallpaper. Two months later, we rented it out. And then we were free.

Really, *really* free. We'd both quit our jobs. This wasn't a two-week honeymoon somewhere hot. I wanted our first year of married life to feel different, to be suitably life-changing, to be an adventure that we shared. I'd already had so many adventures on my own. Our honeymoon would be a year living and working our way around New Zealand, with a bit of backpacking in my beloved Thailand en route.

So what I euphemistically referred to as a 'honeymoon' was

in fact a concerted operation to turn Sean into a traveller. I used all my knowledge of travel, both personally and professionally accrued, to select destinations that I knew to be irresistible, and rewarding, but also not a huge culture shock challenge. Entry-level intrepid travel, basically. Thailand was the first course, to be followed up by an eight-week campervan jaunt around New Zealand, and after that, well, we'd find work in New Zealand if we could, or bugger off to the next stop on our round-the-world tickets. I spent ages plotting the perfect world tour for beginners/people who think they don't like travel. I knew I could make enough money by writing on the road – for *Glamour*, *Grazia*, *Cosmo* and *The Times* – but we also had working visas for both Australia and New Zealand. I'd be lying if I said I hadn't day-dreamed about finding our place, and never coming home. Or getting addicted to life on the road in our campervan, acquiring a cat and a couple of surfboards and never ever settling down with a house.

We had two weeks in Thailand, where Sean sort of enjoyed himself, although he made the rookie error of believing he could take on mosquitos and emerge from South East Asia unbit-ten, victorious. As most of us know, you can't beat mosquitos. Humans can only hope to minimise the horrors of our bloody defeat with balms, lotions, swathes of netting, smoke and spells. And occasionally splat one against our thigh like a tiny blood-filled water bomb, just to make ourselves feel a bit better about being treated like a rolling buffet table by these tiny, buzzing victors. Sean didn't understand this, and charged valiantly into battle with mosquitos, trying to seal up the windows of our beach shacks with rolled towels and dousing himself in DEET, so that when I kissed him on the neck I lost all the feeling in my lips for approximately three hours. He checked our bedding for tiny snipers before tucking the mosquito net so tightly under the mattress that we were sleeping in a wigwam. And, of course, despite all this, we'd both come back from dinner with a few nibbles on our ankles, or wake up in the morning with welts on our forearms. Having lived in Singapore, I was used to this. Sean, however, was outraged.

Flip flops were also a challenge. 'They just keep flying off the end of my feet!' he raged. I did a slow demonstration walk in my own Havaianas, establishing that I did a little grippy motion with my toes, and together we worked through a few sessions of physiotherapy until Sean had mastered the art. Sean found the Thai attitude to timekeeping maddening, and could never quite relax on a bus or a train until he had asked five people if we were definitely on the right one. Much as I try to avoid gender stereotypes, I do allow myself the luxury of this one: I'm firmly of the belief that women make the best travellers.

Men are less comfortable with chaos and therefore suffer more severely from culture shock. Women, on the other hand, eat chaos for breakfast. We devour chaos on toast. And men are oddly reluctant to ask for help or support, while women are unafraid and impatient enough to grab someone and demand directions rather than digging our iPhones out of our bags. But the biggest difference between male and female travellers, generally speaking, is that women fully understand the importance of forging close bonds quickly. Our survival has depended on this for centuries.

Today women are now more likely than men to go it alone,

with females constituting 58 per cent of single travellers, the figure rising for more active and intrepid trips such as walking holidays (64 per cent) and safaris (60 per cent). Increasingly, we're Instagram-obsessed aspirational over-achievers with seriously high demands of our limited leisure time. And, unfairly but unarguably, female travellers have a sense of urgency relating to our careers and family plans that men simply don't. We feel very, very grateful to be travelling. We know that our mothers couldn't have travelled as we do, and that our travels today are beyond the wildest dreams of our grandmothers. Women make very, very grateful travellers. Men have been able to take it for granted for generations.

Women also travel for different reasons from men. For most of us, the real adventure when we travel takes place within, an inner adventure in response to a change in our external circumstances. Women don't travel simply to explore new destinations; we also want to explore new corners of our character, challenge ourselves and embark upon an emotional journey as well as a physical one. Sean was discovering new depths to his grumpiness and unrest, new insects to find irksome, and finding my enjoyment of the whole thing completely alienating. 'You seem to find novelty a virtue in itself,' he said. 'But something can be new or unfamiliar, and still be SHIT.'

We decided to move on to New Zealand.

The standard joke about Brits travelling to New Zealand is that it is like Scotland, only further. But this is precisely the appeal of New Zealand. It's a potent cocktail of the comfortingly familiar and the thrillingly exotic. Wooden Victorian villas with dainty rose gardens, sitting coyly in the shade of a buxom palm tree. Rugged cliffs that look plucked from the west coast of Scotland, looming over volcanic black sand beaches. The alpine angles of Mount Cook, its solitary slopes resembling a child's drawing of a single mountain amid low-lying plains, rather than the jagged rows we have in Europe. And there's the intermingling of towns with twee British colonial names – Wellington and Queenstown – next to ravishing Maori place names like Whakatāne, Rangitoto Island and Taupo. Fish and chip shops abound, but I always ordered mine with a side of *kumara* (sweet potato) fries. Our Kiwi friends got every British cultural reference point going – they'd all grown up watching The Magic Roundabout and Inspector Gadget – to the point where it was eerily easy to forget that they'd grown up on the other side of the world. But I stifled a laugh when fish and chips, pie and lamb with mint sauce were all claimed as Kiwi culinary classics. I always enjoyed telling them, obnoxiously, that the only genuine innovation in Kiwi cooking – something truly original and endemic – was onion dip (ingredients: one packet of powdered onion soup, with one carton of cream, served with a massive bag of crisps).

That's not to say food wasn't a complete joy in New Zealand. As you'd expect from a nation with European and Asian culinary influences and the phenomenal, growing potential of the South Pacific, mealtimes in New Zealand were a highlight. But it was the adoption and adaptation of imported dishes that made it such a treat. Walking down K-Road in Auckland, you can buy Danish bread, eat impeccable sushi and scoff British pub grub. And we revelled in Auckland's breakfast culture, because breakfast is an art form in Auckland. I once interviewed a Kiwi chef who moaned about the limitations of Kiwi cuisine, muttering despondently, 'we've never really gone beyond the BLAT' (bacon, lettuce, avocado, tomato). But to me, breakfasting seemed both glamorous and glossily wholesome. I never ordered a flat white and eggs benny at Kokako without feeling like a celebrity in LA's Silver Lake, a mystery blonde in Lululemon gear hiding behind massive sunglasses and laughing at James Franco's crap jokes. And this hip and healthy breakfast culture allowed Kiwis to tick the social box in their weekend bright and early, and get on with a day of surfing, tramping (that's walking, to anyone else) or dog-wrangling. Meeting for dinner seemed sort of square, by comparison.

If nations could have therapy (which might not be a bad idea), colonialism would come up pretty regularly. In Europe, New Zealand enjoys a sparkling reputation as a natural, wholesome, healthy, beautiful and genetically superior mixed-race stepsister. This isn't how New Zealand sees herself. New Zealand is that girl at school who didn't realise how beautiful, funny, smart and charming she is. The one who could be found self-harming in the toilets rather than queening it up over the popular girls. Her inner voice mutters on about how she's an illegitimate outsider, lesser educated, unsophisticated and embarrassingly gauche – with dorky freckles and a weird gap between her teeth.

What Antipodean sociologists refer to as 'cultural cringe' baffled me. To my mind, New Zealand has nothing whatsoever to cringe about. Being Irish, I felt as if cringing was *my* bag. Strangely, the fact that I'd been writing for British papers – the *Guardian*, the *Independent*, the *Sunday Times* and the *Daily Telegraph* – immediately made me seem more cultured and sophisticated than I actually was. As someone who is pretty good at cringing with perceived inadequacy herself, I found this a very odd position to be in.

Happily, in recent years, New Zealand has perked up, though. Heavyweight cultural exports like *The Lord of the Rings*, *Flight of the Conchords* and Lorde have helped, as must the endless parade of wide-eyed European travellers who love the country so much they cry when they leave.

I arrived a little less wide-eyed than most, as a whore to cities. As one Kiwi friend said, 'Nobody comes to New Zealand for the cities.' When you subject yourself to the twenty-six-hour flight from England to New Zealand, you're doing it with one vision in mind: a holiday immersed in nature, dunked by the ankles into the wilderness. You want to bungee jump into the stuff. I was less excited by this prospect, but, after all, this trip wasn't about me. I was playing the long game. New Zealand was about turning Sean into a traveller, so I had an adventure travel plus-one for life. This is what a husband meant, to me. I felt that the best way to do this was to drag him to the outdoorsy, bucolic land of his dreams, and let New Zealand work her magic.

As a restless, active traveller who loves exploring cities on foot or by bike, campervanning wasn't my natural milieu either, but I knew New Zealand was a destination that rewards visitors who get out on the open road. This is a sparsely populated nation of outdoorsy boy and girl racers, and highways are fringed with cool cafés serving the aforementioned brilliant breakfasts, picnic spots and rustic $5 Department of Conservation campsites, trails off into the forest and quirky B&Bs, markets, shops, vineyards and towns that wouldn't be seen dead on the main highway. Road-tripping is a way of life here in New Zealand, so we loaded up our Spotify playlist, scribbled all over the DOC map of campsites, stocked up on RJ's liquorice and hit the road.

I had organised a series of outdoorsy treats for Sean and me, as I saw them. I fell in love with the bohemian town of Matakana, just an hour north of Auckland, which is essentially a trade show for the good life available in New Zealand. A jazz quartet played Ella Fitzgerald, children were enjoying themselves on the rope swing, couples on first dates nibbled whitebait fritters and debated what foreign movie to catch at the local indie cinema. Matakana is where Auckland's creative classes escape to when they've had enough, to sip organic Feijoa bubbly from the Lothlorien Winery, stock up on raw almond butter from Nuts About NZ and feast on slow-cooked polenta with roast aubergine from We Love Food. This was how I liked the countryside: an edit of the best stuff about the city, with some nice foliage garnishing the edges.

Suitably seduced, we drove north up the coast to Tutukaka, where Sean learned to scuba dive and I dived daily in the weed-rich, highly nutritious waters of the North Island. Essentially this is sea soup, so full of nutrients and fish that shark attacks are vanishingly rare; the sharks have already had all the fish suppers they can handle. We drove south to Raglan, and spent a few days working as teepee attendants at a dreamy surf camp called Solscape. We visited wineries in Hawke's Bay, and then further south in Martinborough, where we watched AC/DC having a long, boozy lunch accompanied by a series of fine vintages. Rock and roll is not dead, but it's certainly grown up.

Being easily bored, what I really need from a road trip is variety of scenery, and happily New Zealand offered an ever-changing, positively fickle, landscape. We weren't far north of Christchurch when the rolling hills of Canterbury's wine region – the Waipara Valley – gave way to the more dramatic peaks of the Southern Alps, as we headed inland towards the spa resort of Hanmer Springs. The next morning we wound our way along the rugged east coast, where the Southern Alps meet the Pacific Ocean. Kaikoura is firmly on the tourist map; what nobody tells you is that the drive might just be the best bit . . . 180km north of Christchurch, on the east coast of New Zealand's South Island, Kaikoura is a town that developed as a centre for the whaling industry and today owes its livelihood to the more gentle sport of whale-watching – from the air, the sea or the many tramping trails in the surrounding mountains.

Most visitors skip the west coast of the South Island because it adds serious kilometres, but we were in the mood for solitude, so we drove towards Westport via the Buller Gorge on Highway 6, where we stopped off to walk the swing bridge, a far better way to inhale your surroundings than the touristy jet boats. The beaches of the west coast were deserted, dramatic and driftwood-dotted, but cursed by sandflies, which made Thailand's mosquitos seem downright benevolent. We jumped and twitched around in our jandals (the Kiwi term for flip flops) as we lit a fire, then gave up and watched the sun go down through the window from the comfort of our campervan, drinking Marlborough Pinot Noir from plastic tumblers – the way it's meant to be enjoyed, I suspect.

We were in no real hurry to reach Fox Glacier (I know glaciers to be overcrowded, grubby things) and so we lingered in the goldmine heritage town of Greymouth (the end of the TranzAlpine railway line from Christchurch) and walked the old railway lines and mining tunnels of the Hokitika Gorge, drinking in the lush vegetation and marvelling at the pioneer spirit that inspired 2013 Man Booker Prize-winner Eleanor Catton's *The Luminaries*. Today Hokitika is more famous for grub than gold, and the annual WildFoods Festival every March should be added to every gung-ho foodie's bucket list.

Franz Josef and Wanaka beckoned, but, again, the journey proved my favourite bit. Crossing the Haast River and working our way inland via the Haast Pass, a World Heritage Area, we realised that road-trip scenery doesn't get much more dramatic than this, so jumped out for a walk on some roadside trails. Wanaka could wait. When we eventually hit town, on a recommendation from a local grocer, we drove out towards Mount Aspiring from Wanaka. When the tarmac ran out, we exhaled – and kept on going into our own little slice of wilderness, for a day of mountain-biking with not a tour bus in sight.

The road to Queenstown served as an advert for coming attractions, with a magnificent scenic drive over the Crown Range, and down to the shores of Lake Wakatipu. We pulled into town – and then pulled out again, to find a campsite fifteen minutes outside town. We'd become accustomed to having New Zealand to ourselves, I guess, and didn't want to share a town with a bunch of bungee-obsessed twenty-one-year-old Australians.

Most visitors do a quick skydive in Queenstown then make a

beeline for Milford Sound, but Sean was craving some Highland scenery and we got a tip from a fellow campervanner that the road out to Glenorchy is an overlooked treat. It was genuinely uncanny – I felt like we were driving north of Fort William in the Scottish Highlands – until I spotted a subtropical giveaway like a palm tree or a fruit orchard. Watching the scenery speed past, choosing picnic spots from the roadside buffet on offer, making sharp turns onto dirt roads that look too enticing to ignore – this was the sort of freedom we bought our campervan for. In New Zealand, my highlights were the bits along the way.

ROAD TRIP RULES

I've road-tripped around California, New Zealand, Scotland, Canada and Italy, and I learned these four rules the hard way, by not following them and having a rubbish time. Don't be me!

1. Try to avoid drives of longer than four hours in a single day. Four hours is just about manageable in a morning, afternoon or chunk of a day, but somehow five hours is the tipping point. Drive for five hours and you feel like you've done nothing but drive all bloody day.

2. Don't make every night a one-night stand. By spending each night in a different place, you miss out on the joy of waking up somewhere and knowing you have all day there, and you don't need to hastily pack your bag before breakfast. It's

far better to cover a smaller area and really relish it than cover a lot of ground but feel like you're just passing through.

3. Make every pit stop count. Try to plan your detours for petrol, supplies shopping and mealtimes around something interesting or beautiful. Whether I travel by road, bike or rail, I always try to make the journey part of the trip, by plotting scenic detours for picnics or stop at farmers' markets or gastropubs along the way. This means my holiday starts the moment I set off.

4. Crowdsource campsite, pub and B&B recommendations by asking on Twitter or Facebook. I also use location-sensitive apps and sites like Cruncho, Yelp, TripAdvisor and Spotted By Locals to make sure I never stop for a sandwich somewhere crummy, when there could be a cute café just a few miles down the road.

Much to my surprise I was in my element here in New Zealand, despite it being pretty much all countryside. I settled comfortably into the simplicity of campervan living, relishing the life edit it had forced us to do. Even my wardrobe had been simplified; I found myself wondering if part of the contentment I felt on the road in our campervan was freedom from all the clutter and miscellaneous stuff that smothered me back home. I got addicted to this simplicity, and imagined taking our van, Lucy (a Toyota Lucida, you see), overseas, eventually winding up in Morocco with two tangle-haired children and a pet parrot.

But Sean, well, he gets the opposite of itchy-footed. He gets distressed by all the motion. Not just the motion. All this relentless *leisure*. 'I feel pointless,' he said, pointedly, at one point.

One of the great luxuries of being a writer is that it permits me to travel anywhere with a sense of purpose. As long as I bring my curiosity and a notepad with me, I am effectively working, banking observations and experiences. Much like fishing is really just an excuse to sit still and hang out alone with some water, and golf is just a reason to go for a walk in the country, so writing allows me to travel incessantly without guilt. No experience, not even a mundane or actively unpleasant one, is a waste; they all wind up in words at some point.

Sean, however, is a sound engineer and has always worked physically, with tangible results at the end of the day – a performance had been completed, sound had been heard. 'I hear the music I mix on this Midas Heritage, therefore I am.' Having nothing to show for himself at the end of the day, well, it threw him. Happily, I had a plan. My friend Laura had lived and worked in New Zealand for a year as a doctor. 'You can fuck on beaches in New Zealand. There is nobody there' was her main travel tip, but she also bought me a year's membership to WWOOF.

Stating that you're a WWOOFer provokes one of two reactions. Either a look of alarm, as if you've just confessed to a niche sexual predilection they're going to have to Google when they get home, or a smile of delighted recognition, because they've been a member of World Wide Opportunities on Organic Farms themselves, or they know someone who has worked in exchange for bed and board on a cute organic farm in Greece.

Some people do it because they're considering a new career in agriculture, others to get a cultural experience, but most of us, let's be honest, do it in order to keep our costs down and prolong a holiday. Getting your bed and board in exchange for four to five hours of being a farmer each day feels like a pretty sweet deal to me.

And I had the address of one particular farm in Gisborne. I believe in travelling with flexible plans, but I also believe in really, really doing your research beforehand if you want to avoid doing something shit. Before I visit a hotel or a destination for work, I double-check sources and recommendations, I read every single grammatically disastrous and intolerably pompous TripAdvisor review, I ring up other journalists (never email, because I want the TRUTH, and no sane journalist tells the whole, unadulterated and potentially libellous truth in an email) and ask for the lowdown.

The WWOOF website these days presents a challenge to someone as obsessive as me, because it's essentially a swamp of job adverts, ranging from corporate chancers cashing in on cultural ignorance and youthful shyness to adorable, homely organic farms where they just can't wait to hear all about life back in Scotland. This was essentially our honeymoon, and I wasn't going to fuck around with the former. So when the couple we bought our campervan off enthused about an organic orange orchard in Gisborne, I took notes. And now, three months on, we nervously rolled up in the yard. Nervous because Sean isn't good at sharing space with other people. I would happily live in a hippy commune and raise other people's children while they took an afternoon off to go and take acid in the forest, if I could only find the right crew. Whereas Sean, well, nothing ruins Sean's day like a social plan in the evening.

'If they're weird, or wankers, or work us too hard, we can just do a midnight flit,' I whispered reassuringly, as a beaming retired couple, Jasper and Judy, arrived at the door and offered to help us with our rucksacks, before sitting us down and presenting us with freshly baked scones.

We'd struck WWOOFing gold with Jasper and Judy. Our mornings started at six o'clock, when we sipped a quick coffee, then worked for two hours, then took a break for a breakfast on the porch before working for another two hours and finally winding up at lunchtime. Our afternoons were our own. And the hours out in the orchards flew by.

I found the combination of satisfying, tangible, physical work in the outdoors the perfect contrast and counterbalance to writing. Being a writer is a brilliant career, a curiosity-sating, ego-stroking, mentally challenging job that brings me into contact with the best and brightest of people, the word's movers and shakers. I get to be a tourist in other people's worlds, spending New York Fashion Week with Kyra Kennedy and Tiffany Trump, driving through the Arctic Circle with ice-road truckers, hanging out with gorilla trackers and wildlife wardens in Rwanda – then moving on to the next assignment, a whole new world.

But there is no escaping the physical reality of writing: this job essentially requires me to sit on my arse staring at a screen for up to twelve hours a day, jacked up on caffeinated drinks and in a state of manufactured anxiety, oscillating between manic grandiosity and crippling self-doubt, mainlining carbs and trying desperately to steer myself away from sobbing over other people's perfect families on Facebook or buying vintage curtains on eBay. Oh, and failing to wash because you're always about to go for a run, or about to go and do some yoga, or you're about to walk to the shop, but these things that are always about to happen never actually do happen. Writing is a wonderful career, but in no way is it healthy. And I've spent much of my life outside work desperately trying to mitigate the ill effects of my job. Perhaps we all do.

But being half-farmer, half-writer struck me as just the right balance, a nourishing career cocktail. I could perch on a bale of hay, interviewing a celebrity on Skype for *Glamour* magazine. While I prattled on about how this was the ideal portfolio career for me, Sean stayed silent, but there was a more profound change taking place inside him, a realisation that he was happiest outdoors, working with plants. A realisation that would eventually lead to him ditching his fun-but-even-unhealthier-than-writing career as a live sound engineer, to become a gardener at the Royal Horticultural Society. It would take Sean another few years to fully process this, because that is his way. I, meanwhile, change course with all the alacrity of a pinball, and I'd decided that I was officially outdoorsy.

Part of my new love of the outdoors stems directly from gluttony. I grew up in the 1990s, in the heyday of supermarket ready meals, eating crap mass-farmed fruit and veg packaged in plastic. So the novelty of picking a fig from a tree and popping it straight in my mouth was a real thrill for me.

I had already started to relish the simplicity of campervan living, but now I realised that this less-is-more approach rang true for both the contents of my soap bag *and* my social life. In London, the dizzying array of shows and plays and supper clubs and new restaurant openings made me feel panicky and a little bit overwhelmed, horror-struck that I was missing out. In Gisborne, our weekly outing to the local cinema on Friday felt like a total cultural treat, a well-earned indulgence. I'd spent my afternoons surfing the waves, or writing articles for *Grazia*, *Condé Nast Traveller* and the *Guardian*, as I sat among the fig trees, and a movie felt like a decadent and intellectual feast. I found that with less going on around me, I was motivated to do more. I auditioned for a local low-budget vampire movie, and played the role of a concerned teacher who realises, to her alarm, that LOCAL KIDS ARE GOING MISSING. My scenes were shot after a morning picking oranges.

But the thing that really got me about New Zealand? Waking up every morning surrounded by beauty. And before I knew what was happening, waking up somewhere beautiful became a non-negotiable for me. I didn't want to live a ninety-minute drive from somewhere beautiful. I wanted beauty on my doorstep. Or a short walk or bike ride away. Living in Hackney, I woke up surrounded by excitement, sure. But I had to plan an outing to beauty, or tell myself that next weekend, if I was good, I might get some beauty. Hackney's well-meaning parks and marshes didn't quite do it for me. Having lived in Northern Ireland and Scotland, I have high standards for my countryside, and half-assed southern English countryside can just go home. In New Zealand, living out of a campervan, I realised that natural beauty is a gift, and it's a gift I don't believe in rationing. It's not like booze, or sugar, or angry music, or other treats that you might need to limit in the name of health. The more natural beauty you get, the better you get.

And just like that, London, my favourite city in the world, lost its power over me. It wasn't beautiful enough. Some cities around the world do offer extravagant natural beauty as well as the cultural swagger and architectural heft of a city. Glasgow has Loch Lomond less than half an hour away. Vancouver is famous for offering the best of both worlds; you can surf and snowboard the same day, you're always told, although what sort of wanker would try to do both, rather than heading to the pub after one? Seattle, San Francisco, Cape Town, Manchester – the list goes on.

But London, London was not placed where it is, centuries ago, with any thought for the lifestyle needs of millennials. Those early settlers were thinking more about Roman roads and waterways and crap like that, rather than proximity to immersive experiences and the availability of adrenalin-fuelled sports and other essential accoutrements of our eternal quest for work–life balance.

I remember once getting the bus into London from Glasgow and staring out of the window, noting with excitement that we appeared to be nearing the city centre, because we were plainly on the high street – there were giveaway signs like a Boots store and an HSBC. I was in Ealing. We were still over an hour from Victoria Coach Station. 'London is ALL main road,' I told my friends back in Glasgow, giving them no indication at all that I'd one day specialise in observational travel writing.

I started to realise that I'd taken the outdoorsy charms of Britain for granted. It was ridiculous that I now knew New

Zealand better than Ireland, Scotland or England, the countries I have called home. And city life, well, city life in London, it would never be enough for me ever again. When we left New Zealand after three months on the farm in Gisborne, I did so with a new-found appreciation for natural beauty, and a sense that I'd rather live somewhere beautiful, somewhere that was a good, wholesome influence on me, and then plan thrilling weekends in the big city, than the other way around. It felt a bit like the realisation that you don't actually want your most hedonistic friend as your flatmate. You want to live with the PhD student who goes to the gym and washes the dishes after her. And you want your chain-smoking, hilarious but wild mate to be waiting for you in the pub. I was ready to move on from London. I would see her in the pub.

8

Amalfi Coast: Making Life Sweet Again

One thing I adore about travel is that when you step off the flight, you're stepping into a whole new you. Or, better still, you're stepping *out* of the old you. Nobody knows if you've just been dumped, been sacked, or if you've left a trail of wanton destruction behind you. You can book a £5 pedicure, plonk yourself on a yoga mat, book a few surf or dive lessons and – abrakebabra – you're a whole new person. Travel is the ultimate self-help intervention; meditation can go jump. I've regularly used travel to fix myself. And there has been quite a lot to fix. I've had to travel a LOT, and I've barely made a dent in my internal chaos.

Throughout my life, I've experienced bouts of depression, some of them fairly serious. My symptoms are always the same. Depression feels to me like sinking, day by day and week by week, moods getting a little lower, the light more distant, human connection further out of reach. I refuse to call it by its full name until one day I realise I'm completely submerged.

At the age of thirty-one, I found myself slipping under. When Sean decided to retrain in horticulture, I suggested that we move back into my old student flat in Glasgow to save money. I knew I loved Glasgow, we had a crew of hilarious and hedonistic friends there, and ten years in crap shared flats in London had made me come to view my student flat in Partick as a vaulted-ceilinged grand palace with cavernous chambers of storage for clothes.

Sean could volunteer at the Botanical Gardens, and I'd write the novel I'd always dreamed of. Writing a book was a project which essentially required me to create more hours in my working day, since I was still working full-time as a freelance journalist. For the next six months, I resolved to get up at six every morning and do three hours of work on the book before my normal working day began. It would be tough, but we've all been there – knowing we need to buckle down and focus 100 per cent on a crucial work project, an exam or a job interview.

In truth, I was quite excited about this 'work bootcamp', or 'Project Book' as I jokingly called it to friends. The language of motivational self-help books floated through my mind: I would be a highly effective person! I'd be firing on all cylinders! I'd be at the top of my game! Yes, this extreme work schedule would mean cutting down on boozy nights out with my mates, but it would be worth it. And this would *not* be like my final exams at university, where I fuelled late-night cramming sessions with Nescafé and Boost bars, and paid for my first-class degree with an extra stone of weight, bad skin and depression.

Now I was older, and (I thought) wiser. I would eat well. I'd get eight hours' sleep every night. I'd ditch coffee. I would go out for a run or a yoga class every day. I would do *everything* right. What could possibly go wrong? Quite a lot, it turns out.

Years ago, as a boozy twenty-seven-year-old, I'd given up drinking for six months. Sean had decided his drinking was a problem, which I think it was, and I wanted to support him kick a destructive habit, rather than blithely getting pissed on prosecco while he sat next to me battling inner demons. Although giving up drinking didn't change my life, it didn't ruin it either. And I came through the other side with a new-found ability: I could refuse those free glasses of wine at a boring work function, I could sip elderflower cordial at a Sunday afternoon barbecue, I could draw a line after three whiskies in the pub. I learned to say no, the hardest word in the world.

The first time I went booze-free I was working in the *Grazia* office in London, so was still out most nights with work buddies, simply drinking a fauxito instead of a mojito. Now I was working from my old student flat in Glasgow, gazing out of the window at the January rain. This time I hadn't just cut down on my alcohol intake, I'd given up going out at all. To get my requisite 'eight hours' I needed to be in bed by 10 p.m., so even my regular Wednesday night trip to the cinema with friends was ruled out.

Even so, I expected to be feeling brilliant. Who doesn't think that if they grant themselves eight hours of sleep, regular exercise sessions, no booze and healthy eating, that they'll uncover previously untapped reserves of energy, unleash their creativity and generally take their lives to the next level?

However, at the six-week mark I realised I wasn't feeling particularly brilliant. I could feel the familiar old niggle of depression. Desperate to keep it at bay, I became even more disciplined in my regime. I started getting up at 5.30 a.m. so I could have an 'endorphin-boosting' run in the park before starting work at 6.30 a.m. I'd read that sugar and caffeine can cause mood swings, so I cut them out entirely. My evenings were spent either in front of the TV or at a yoga class. My bootcamp mentality was now just as much about beating depression as about the book.

By this stage, I barely saw my friends apart from the occasional coffee (in the figurative sense, that is; I sipped mint tea) with a friend on a Saturday morning. My social life was confined to Twitter and Facebook, those bastions of poor self-esteem and degenerating mental health.

By this stage I felt so low that I didn't feel like seeing anyone anyway, so it barely registered as something that might be wrong. Sean knew I was stressed and unhappy, but his gentle suggestions that I 'take it easy for a while' or 'loosen up' were met with swift rebuttals. Didn't he understand that I had a book to write? The worst thing was that my creativity had completely dried up. I was at my desk for twelve hours a day, but I wasn't making any progress on my book. Furious at myself, I responded by banning alcohol entirely.

'I don't understand it, I've been doing *everything* in my power to keep depression at bay,' I told Sean one morning, through hot, frustrated tears. 'All I *do* is go to sodding yoga classes and make stupid salad lunches. I couldn't be trying any *harder.*'

I didn't realise that something had been helping me which I'd taken for granted: fun. I hadn't had fun for months. I'd hardly seen my friends. I hadn't seen anything interesting at all. But I still couldn't see that not drinking had made me more stressed, not less. What had started as a small goal became enormous in my mind – a level of perfection I must maintain.

I know it seems bananas, but it never occurred to me that this strict regime might have been contributing to how bad I was feeling. Some of you will be thinking, 'Er, of *course* such a puritanical schedule would make you miserable. Where's your common sense?' Others, because of the job you do, the stuff you read, or simply the sort of person you are, will understand how easily the twenty-first-century pressure to be at your best can spiral into obsession. We're constantly being told that eliminating things – late nights, wheat, sugar, dairy, alcohol, caffeine – is a good thing. My knee-jerk response to feeling bad – emotionally, mentally or physically – was to cut something out.

At the three-month point I started experiencing panic attacks when I went outside, twitching and muttering angrily to myself in Tesco, like the sort of person you'd choose a longer queue in order to avoid. By this stage I had left it too late. Too late for medication that would take a fortnight to kick in. Too late to combat it with the endorphins of exercise, good food and upbeat company. By now, these weapons had been kicked to the other side of the room, far out of my reach. And now that I was submerged, it took me hours to get out of the door in the morning, because fits of tears and despondency set me back forty-five minutes at a time. I would have stayed in bed all day if I could – and I'm normally one of those jerks who can brag about being a 'morning person'.

I'd wake up with a raging thirst for crisps and chocolate, and a lump of sadness ready-prepared in my throat. Any minor mishap or inconvenience – spilling a cup of (decaf) coffee, my phone battery dying – became a metaphor for my entire miserable existence. The world assumed the cast of a grisly cartoon scene; a Hogarth picture without the comfort of drunkenness. Everything my eyes landed on was just more evidence that life is grim and hopeless; I saw everything through sludge-grey tinted spectacles.

When you're depressed, everyday life feels like an assault course, every errand, interaction or place a potential pitfall, the thing that will set you off, provoke an undignified, shrieking meltdown. It could be something as inconsequential as a trashy pop track blaring in Pret, but it will induce a full-blown, hyper-ventilating, twitching, shouting, tearful panic attack.

If all this sounds melodramatic, of course it is. Melodrama is depression's one saving grace. Thinking of overblown and verbose ways to describe how crap you feel is the only thing that gets us through. Without words, or music, or art, or film, we'd be completely screwed.

Along with the classic symptoms – food cravings, lack of motivation, difficulty getting out of bed and an overwhelming, inescapable feeling of despair, the most distressing signs of my own bespoke depression were the violent fantasies. 'I, well, the thing is – I just can't stop thinking about stabbing myself in the face.' That's how I put it to my GP when I was a student in Glasgow, the first doctor I ever spoke to about it.

And, yes, my thoughts definitely turned to suicide, too. If there was a way of painlessly and quietly editing myself out of the world, I would have done it years ago. The pain I refer to is the pain of others, by the way. Depression hurts, a lot more than suicide. Every inhalation is a gasp of horror, every exhalation a sigh of resignation.

Fortunately, my exit route has always been different. It's been travel. Travel has never failed me. Most winters I feel the black dog snapping at my heels, and over the years I've developed a series of rules, strategies and steps to avoid it. Because I have always been the weather's bitch. And, after years of mulling it over, I've come to the conclusion that the only real difference between the seasonal depression I've experienced and regular, bog-standard depression isn't one of degree; it's its weak point, how you can hit it where it hurts and tackle it to the ground. With SAD (seasonal affective disorder) I always nursed a conviction that sunshine and warmth would burn the gloom off. That if I could just stretch my arms above me and shove a few clouds out of the way, my mood would soar, and I'd soon pop up for air, gulping gratefully. With non-seasonal depression, wasting the sunshine because you can't get out of bed is just one more thing to feel bad about.

EMOTIONAL JOURNEYS

Travel trends are a reliable barometer of any society; what we daydream giddily about and demand of our downtime tells us a hell of a lot about what's lacking in our daily lives. With 18-hour digital working days, soul-crushing commutes, desk-shackled existences, financial pressure and constant sensory over-stimulation, it's perhaps no surprise that young travellers are rediscovering the walking holiday, the pilgrimage, the lone odyssey on foot.

▶

Centuries ago, humans recognised the redemptive value of endurance walking for personal and spiritual growth. Surviving descriptions of Christian pilgrimages to the Holy Land date back to the 4th century, when pilgrimage was encouraged by church figures such as Saint Jerome, and established by Helena, mother of Constantine the Great. The pilgrimage to Mecca is one of the Five Pillars of Islam, to be attempted at least once in the lifetime of all able-bodied Muslims with the means to do so. Solitude, reflection, simplicity, the removal of distractions and a healthy dose of hardship were tools that turned boys into men, toughened us up, cleansed our souls and brought us back to ourselves.

By the 18th century, wilderness walking wasn't purely undertaken for spiritual or religious reasons, but for creative, artistic and personal reasons too. Perhaps most famously, the English Romantic poets who I adore – Wordsworth, Coleridge and Shelley – recognised the redemptive, healing powers of the natural world: they were pioneers of a 'back to nature' creative mentality. Nature never failed Wordsworth; he'd go on lengthy walks in the Lake District, return, and pick up his pen. Walking and writing have always had an intimate relationship, because walking is inspiration, walking is observation, and walking is a healing process.

Walking holidays *work* for the simplest of reasons: beautiful surroundings, a sense of achievement, and endorphin-boosting physical activity. But as any seasoned hiker knows, there's some magic to a walking adventure that can't be quantified, that psychologists are only starting to unpick – and apply to our productivity at work, stress levels and personal relationships. Back in the 1970s, University of Michigan psychologists Rachel and Stephen Kaplan distinguish between two forms of attention: 'directed attention', i.e. the forced concentration of our working day, versus 'fascination'. Today we suffer from 'directed attention fatigue' and the impulsivity, distractibility and irritability that accompany it. The remedy? Spending time amidst nature, where our brains are engaged automatically by beautiful surroundings. 'Directed attention fatigues people through overuse,' explains Stephen. 'If you can find an environment where the attention is automatic, you allow directed attention to rest. And that means an environment that's strong on fascination.'

Don't think I'm not aware how immensely privileged I am to have travel as a relief valve for my depression. It's an escape hatch that isn't open to everyone – we have financial barriers, family commitments and countless other things. But it's no accident that I do. I deliberately set my life up in a way that kept this escape hatch open. I got used to travelling solo, because when a girl needs a trip a girl needs a trip. I've only had relationships with people who got that I needed my independence and wouldn't take it personally if I buggered off for a week on my own. And it's why I've postponed having children for as long as possible. I also chose to go freelance; one major factor in this decision was that I found the long winter months commuting from Hackney to Covent Garden a slog, and I wanted to be able to work from somewhere sunny if my moods started to take on a darker hue.

I finally went to see the doctor and was prescribed Citalopram, and was told to come back in a fortnight. But during this fortnight was a week I'd been dreading. Typing these words now, it sounds ridiculous that I ever dreaded a week in Italy with old friends from New Zealand, a blisteringly funny couple called Jo and Konrad, who both work in TV. But I did, because this week meant alcohol (a banned substance in my life), it meant carbs (surely I'd get an energy slump or low moods?) but, most dreaded of all, it meant lively conversation, social interaction, going outside. In my current state of crippling social anxiety, I felt hopelessly inadequate for the task of being a normal human on holiday.

And, even through the gloom of my depression, I remained a travel snob. I would never have chosen to visit Amalfi in June. 'People in the know' had tutted at my plans and warned me it would be crowded. And I had a travel writer's inverted snobbery about visiting a 'touristy' location. I'd heard that Puglia is the new Tuscany! Everyone's obsessed with Sicily at the moment!

Amalfi is hardly an 'insider's secret', a 'hidden gem', a 'hotspot', an 'emerging destination' or any of those other travel journalism clichés. People have been banging on about how great Amalfi is for centuries, although the coast was once considered a rough diamond, and therefore attracted writers, artists and associated bohemians and hangers-on, a sort of Joshua Tree for early twentieth-century writers. D. H. Lawrence worked on *Lady Chatterley's Lover* in Ravello, and Virginia Woolf and the Bloomsbury set would visit most years, staying at Villa Cimbrone. John Steinbeck visited in 1953, and described it as one of the 'most beautiful and dramatic coastlines in the world', and this was coming from a writer embroiled in a lifelong love affair with California's Pacific Coast. Although he did permit himself a thoroughly Californian observation about the coastal road, observing that it had '1,000 bends' and was 'carefully designed to be a little bit narrower than two cars side by side'. In Ravello's main square there is a plaque commemorating starry Hollywood visitors like Humphrey Bogart, Greta Garbo, John Huston and Truman Capote. Amalfi was already a tourism superstar. I couldn't kid myself that I was making any great discovery here.

But we arrived at our rental villa in little Minori, and I real-ised that all the modern-day tourists and all those dead writers and movie stars, well, they weren't wrong. The Amalfi Coast is about as dramatic and beautiful as Mediterranean landscapes get, with plunging mountains and soaring cliffs, topped off with picturesque pastel-hued towns and dinky harbours. But I felt like a grey girl in a colourful world, oddly out of place in Amalfi.

Our first night, I spotted an amber-hued drink being sipped by glamorous Italian women across the terrace. What could it be? It looked like nuclear Orangina. Perhaps if I sipped all that colour I'd feel a little bit less grey, I thought. And this is how I met Aperol Spritz. I'd arrived in Italy thinking I'd try not to drink, but glimpsed that amber nectar of the gods and thought, 'fuck it', one of my most useful positive mantras when I travel. The perfume-advert-attractive waiter brought me my drink on a tray, the atomic orange hue seared the back of my retinas, and ice cubes tinkled the glass like wind chimes. It was the first time my senses had had anything pleasant to sense in ages. I took my first faintly medicinal sip. There was sun on my skin and the smell of frangipani in the air. My senses were back. I felt, if not quite human, at least animal again.

Waking up in bed the next morning I warned myself that I'd probably feel terrible. But I didn't. I had nice memories of the night before. Eating carbs and drinking aperitivos hadn't dulled my productivity. It hadn't made me unhealthier. I wasn't fatter. I was just happier. I realised that Italy might just be the place to give my soul a makeover. Italy was the prescription I'd needed. I stopped taking the Citalopram.

Jo and Konrad are glorious livers of life, and in New Zealand Jo and I had been fun-loving partners in crime. 'Blonde and fabulous' were her words for us, and even though I had an Irish awkwardness and darkness that she didn't, I could muster up some of her luminosity, her lust for life. Jo and Italy, well, it was lust at first sight. And spending a week with her in Amalfi was essentially an internship with the best, most confident and most dazzling version of myself. Her wide smile, her delight in Italian glamour, her deliciously vicious sense of humour, it all reminded me of what I could be like when I tried. I put on make-up for the first time in weeks. I got into a bikini. And we rented a speedboat and charged around the coastline, like film stars. 'Who ARE we?' laughed Jo, and I laughed back, realising that I hadn't exercised my diaphragm with such raucous laughter in months.

Italy taught me something that week. I had completely and utterly taken the benefits of my social life for granted. I'd thought of my friends and family as a distraction, when in fact they're a very necessary pillar of support. I'd underestimated the importance of fun. Romance. And lust.

For centuries, sexually repressed, gastronomically unadventurous and emotionally retarded British artists and aristocrats have been travelling to Italy and returning transformed. Italy is a powerful tonic that restores our appetites and awakens the senses. Italy, despite what the Italians say, is not really about love. Italy is too set in its ways for that. But Italy is about lust. In Italy, lust is the acceptable face of love. Love is the real danger, the real threat, the seditious, revolutionary force that must be quashed.

No other nation does lust quite like Italy. The architecture flirts and teases, all swirls, curves and angles sculpted with one thing in mind: to halt us in the street, leaving us slack-jawed and wide-eyed. Italian towns are built for pleasure, never practicality, with leafy piazzas and pastel-hued palazzos, now surrounded by traffic jams and chaotic highways.

Italian fashion has always been less about individual style and more about the fine art of showing off. There is safety in expensive labels, and security in bling. Italian style is peacockery, and Italy's unapologetically showy take on fashion is seductive in itself. There is no shame in showing off in Italy, and that very self-assurance is arousing.

Then there is Italy's food and wine. Italian food is all about extracting the maximum amount of pleasure from a few tomatoes or olives. Italian cooks will stop at nothing to make a tomato delicious, exceptional, the best tomato you've ever set tongue on. Their very ardour is thrilling. Italian cuisine is a courtship;

every plate an attempt to seduce. It's irresistible. And it was the perfect prescription for me.

Before we flew, I was still, ridiculously, dreading Italy, worried that Italy's lust for life would merely expose my own impotence. But it didn't. Italy returned me to my senses, it reunited me with my passions, and it fixed me. Travel can't fix everything, I know that. But if you learn to prescribe yourself trips, there is a lot you *can* fix. Italy nudged me in the right direction, when I'd lost my way.

9

Bali: Making Work Work for You

'You're a writer? You're lucky, I guess you can work from *anywhere*.' People say this to me on a near-weekly basis, but, like most things that strangers say to you in the first five minutes, this is absolute bollocks. Yes, I can take my MacBook anywhere. I can email editors my articles from anywhere. But being creative and productive somewhere is something else entirely.

As a reporter sent across the world to be nosy about a specific thing and write about it, I'm used to filing stories from hotel rooms at 4 a.m., ferociously tickling the keypad of my laptop in airport lounges, and desperately seeking out the quiet corners of cafés. And I've become something of a connoisseur (okay, 'fusspot') of working environments. I can list the specific sofas, the cafés and the cities themselves where I find myself inspired and industrious. And I can name the places where working, well, it just doesn't work out for me.

As more and more of us leave conventional office spaces

167

behind, figuring out how to make work work for us is becoming ever more important. I know writers and designers who insist that background music gets their creative juices flowing. Joylessly enough, I can't listen to music and write at the same time. (Technically, I can listen to music without *English* words in it – there's only room in my mind for one set of English words at a time, you see – but this specification makes me sound even more of a neurotic killjoy than if I simply demand silence, so I stick to the blanket ban.) I need some light, but not so much that I feel like a tomato in a greenhouse. I need to *have my back against the wall looking into the room*, like a gangster. Milk cannot be being steamed within ten feet of my eardrums. And I need to find my surroundings vaguely pleasant, so that when I glance up for a screen break I don't find myself immediately depressed and forced on to Refinery29 to look at nice pictures and pretend that this is my glossy world instead for the next twelve hours. A very real worry.

What permits us to work well gets even more complicated when we consider the environment or city beyond our immediate four walls. For a time I felt that as a lifestyle journalist covering new trends in fashion, culture, food and society, I needed to be in one of a cluster of large, big-name, fast-paced cities in the world. A New York, Paris, London or Berlin, where trends move fast, where people queue round the block for a restaurant one weekend and have moved on to the next pop-up the next. Now I know I just need to be somewhere where life is fizzing, where people are doing inspirational things, where I will come into contact with things that excite me and I want to write about. Plenty of smaller towns, such as Provincetown in

Cape Cod, Gisborne in New Zealand and Margate in Kent, do just fine as well. As I've said, my job is simple: to go forth, be nosy and write about the fruits of my nosiness in an engaging and possibly entertaining manner. As long as I have stuff to be nosy about, I'm golden.

This idea of how to make work work for you is important to me, because I got it badly wrong a few years ago. In Glasgow, as I have said, I had sunk into a deep depression and been medicated for periods of agoraphobia. (I know, a travel writer with agoraphobia. I know.) Today I can see what went wrong: I cheerily and unthinkingly abandoned a community of colleagues and friends I'd spent a decade building. I also gave up the more interesting aspects of my job: London-based interviews, quick-fire international assignments and trend stories that took me outside. By moving away from the capital I'd confined myself to desk work, interviewing people via Skype and doing all my research online. My salary remained the same, but my working week faded from Technicolor to monochrome. I got into journalism because I'm curious, I'm social and I'm an insatiable neophiliac desperate to try new things. In Glasgow, because my work didn't take me outside, I didn't really go outside. It was January, it was Glasgow, I was on a budget because my husband had quit work. There was a long list of reasons to stay indoors. So I'd learned a lesson in Glasgow: I can't work from anywhere. The conditions have to be right.

Amalfi helped me pick myself up off the floor, and a few weeks later I moved back to London to work at Vogue House, having gratefully accepted the role of acting deputy editor of

Condé Nast Brides magazine, while my friend Claudia Waterson was on maternity leave. I wasn't that into weddings, but I was into honeymoons and it was my job to look after the travel section. I figured that most sane couples these days see their honeymoon as an intrepid trip of a lifetime, rather than a dull week on a sun lounger in the Maldives. And with Claudia and my editor, Jade, we worked to make sure we covered the coolest, most envy-inducing adventures on the planet. I reviewed pre-wedding yoga breaks, I reviewed batchelorette parties in Las Vegas, and – always the best bit – I reviewed honeymoons, from surfing in Sri Lanka to gorilla-tracking in Rwanda.

Having realised that working from home drives me mad, after I left Vogue House I spent subsequent years working happily in an atmospheric, if slightly ramshackle, co-working space in Hackney called Netil House. My studio, which I shared with Kat, a jewellery designer, Hannah, an arts curator, and Agnes, a photographer, was sandwiched between a posh Pilates studio and a badly run café bar with battered leather sofas, battered creatives and a roof terrace overlooking the railway tracks. We used a sari instead of a curtain, and burned incense to cover up the smell of cigarettes wafting in from the roof terrace. We'd even found a French radio station (no distracting English lyrics) that I could actually tolerate in the background. I was happy there.

But every so often a British winter comes along where it feels like the weather really is working against you. And I've always been prone to taking the weather personally. When a friend (bastard) sent me pictures of a dreamy, steamy bamboo co-working space in Bali, my wanderlust went into overdrive. Hubud, aka 'Hub-in-Ubud', is a bamboo co-working space in Bali, with super-fast Wi-Fi, standing desks and Skype conferencing facilities – oh, and a poolside bar. And monkeys, being minutes from Ubud's famous Monkey Forest. Personally I think that monkeys are overrated (I'm more of an ape girl myself), but I wouldn't hold that against Hubud.

I began to daydream about shifting my laptop to this bamboo workplace of dreams, writing inspired words as I watched the steam rise from a neighbouring paddy field, casually tucking one ankle behind my neck in a morning yoga class before sipping on a hemp smoothie. I couldn't quite afford a holiday, because Sean was retraining and I had to cover the rent and his student fees on my freelance salary, a challenge every single month. But my Irish grandmother, Greta, always said, 'a change is as good as a break'. If the new wave of digital nomads have a mantra, this is it.

When all I need to run my business is a laptop and a Skype headset, what on earth was I doing in Hackney in November? Why put up with the pollution, the urban squalor, the rain and the sky-high rent when I could open my laptop in Thailand, Australia or Germany – and move on to another hot-desking set-up and Airbnb rental when I get bored with the view? Travel remains the ultimate aspiration for this wide-eyed, idealistic generation of mine, and technological and financial circumstances have conspired to give us portable, lightweight lives. In 2012 the digital analyst Mary Meeker identified 'the asset-light generation', alluding to pillars of the sharing economy like Airbnb, Zipcar and Spotify as evidence that young consumers like myself are increasingly concerned with 'access' instead of 'ownership'. Which is handy, because ownership – of homes, cars and other assets – is increasingly a pipe dream for us. But travel? Travel makes us all feel rich.

So one morning, after a rainy cycle to Broadway Market and a £12 smoothie, I secured a commission from the *Daily Telegraph* about digital nomadism, booked my flights and a £20 a night guesthouse in the heart of Ubud, and requested a four-week membership at Hubud. Even within the hip, fast-evolving realm of co-working spaces, Hubud is an outlier – and its 250-strong community believes that this highly covetable office environment is the workplace of the future.

The friend who'd put Hubud tantalisingly on my radar was Hayley Hogan, an Australian fellow writer who'd contacted me after reading a few of my other pieces in the *Telegraph*. We'd bonded online fast and when I arrived in Ubud she and her partner Ivor picked me up in their beaten-up jeep and took me straight to a party full of 'Hubudians'.

Obviously at times like this there is a part of me (say, 99 per cent) that just wants to lie flat on the cool sheets of my bed after a long flight, eating an entire dinner of Frito Lay crisps from 7Eleven. But I am my own bitch boss from hell, and I ordered myself to go forth and be nosy like a good journalist.

I found myself at a vast bamboo villa, part of a thoroughly eclectic mix: wealthy techies from Silicon Valley, broke hippies launching social enterprises, yogis, Bitcoiners, traders. A few years ago, if I'd told editors I was shipping out to Bali for a few weeks they'd have assumed I was off to get stoned on a beach somewhere. But Ubud hasn't been dubbed 'Silicon Bali' for nothing, and tech workers make up the largest demographic. TedxUbud was launched in 2011 and has been running every year since, a major date in the calendar of long-term Hubudians. Initiatives like Livit (liv.it) and Tribewanted (tribewantedbali.strikingly.com) are essentially bootcamps for start-ups, where office space, accommodation and meals are provided. Livit's tagline? 'Where entrepreneurs come together and get shit done.'

In his book *The 4-Hour Work Week: Escape 9–5, Live Anywhere and Join the New Rich*, Tim Ferriss argues for 'lifestyle integration' as an approach to travel, versus the traditional idea of slogging your guts out until you retire and head off on a cruise. To Ferriss's mind, we can work as we travel and distribute what he calls 'mini-retirements' throughout life. In the past, holidays were the opposite of work. But during my working life, this has changed, the lines have blurred and I've been able to write articles about 'workends' and 'paycations'.

Our parents sold themselves on long hours for the dream of retiring at fifty to sail around the world, or owning a five-bedroom home in the country – but these things are about as real as a unicorn to most people born after 1980. And many of us watched our parents bust a gut their entire lives – only to see their hard-built businesses collapse or them be made redundant in the aftermath of the 2008 recession. Money hasn't lost its lustre, but we want to earn it on our own terms, doing something we care about, in surroundings that suit us. And perhaps accompanied by a cold Bintang.

THE LAPTOP LIFESTYLE

As a freelance writer, I've always felt that freedom is one of my greatest career assets, and this flexibility has allowed me to work full-time from a campervan in New Zealand for six months, from beach huts across Thailand, from Hubud in Bali one winter, and from an Airbnb in Los Angeles for six months.

But recently I've noticed that the laptop lifestyle is no longer confined to writers like me – I'm sharing co-working spaces and 'coffices' (yep, that's coffee shops that double as offices) with doctors, CEOs, consultants and designers – professions that would previously have meant inflexible hours and a desk-bound existence. Whether you're a 'digital nomad' running a design business from a laptop as you move from one beach to the next, or whether you simply crave the freedom to work from home in your pyjamas if you choose to, our generation believes that 'work' is a state of mind, not a geographical location that we swipe in and out of.

'Young people want the freedom, as promised by technology and the mobility of social media, to arrange their professional lives around their personal ones, rather than the other way round,' says trend forecaster Zoë Lazarus.

This shift towards a laptop lifestyle, or 'location-independent' employment, has largely been made possible by recent advances in the fields of technology and communications. Skype changed everything for freelancers and forward-thinking business owners; I've interviewed celebrities in LA from a vineyard in New Zealand. For creative collaborations or accountancy, we rely on file-sharing software like GoogleDocs, Delicious, Dropbox and WeTransfer, while Zero enables entrepreneurs to monitor their bank balance in real time, and HootSuite helps small businesses streamline their social media from an iPhone. Google Hangout and Slack bring workers together across borders, eliminating the need for a physical shared workspace. And Nomad List continually score the world's towns cities on how well they cater for digital nomads; Budapest, Berlin and Bangkok are the current hotspots.

Meanwhile, sites such as Upwork or Taskrabbit, that connect freelancers to employers, have made it easy to market yourself as an independent contractor. 'The digital nomad dream is now very much a reality,' says Hayley Connick, UK Country Manager of Upwork, the world's largest freelance talent marketplace. 'Today you can be designing for a client in London or coding for a client in New York while swinging from a hammock in Jamaica. As collaboration and communication technologies advance at lightning speed it's no longer necessary to restrict yourself to work available within commuting distance.' It's a win–win situation: businesses get fast access to quality talent, and skilled freelancers can find a more independent, flexible lifestyle. The benefits for workers – to our bank balance, our stress levels, and our relationships, are clear.

In addition to technological advances, however, there's been a philosophical shift. 'For millennials, money is less relevant; they crave meaning from their career, they want their work to be a mission,' adds Maurits Kalff, a psychologist specialising in people management, and faculty member of London's School of Life. 'The lines between the personal and the professional have blurred, so your job really needs to say something about you.'

Back in our parents' day, people wanted the top job at the biggest company. Today, nobody has that dream. Young professionals no longer fantasise about a big home in the suburbs and being able to afford a nanny – instead we daydream about operating a successful e-commerce business, social enterprise or blogging empire from the kitchen table, with the optional extra of a toddler sleeping peacefully in the next room.

In Ubud, the *Eat, Pray, Love* hippies haven't entirely vacated the premises, but a new wave of Ferriss-inspired, tech-savvy, fiercely driven digital nomads has overtaken Ubud, drawn here by the beauty, the cheap bungalows and the dream of a yoga-hewn, superfood-filled healthy body. And the list of portable professions is growing day by day. I chatted to Dani, a Canadian GP who runs a virtual clinic three times a week, seeing patients all over British Columbia via a Skype-like secure video platform. 'Patients are screened by an assistant beforehand, and I get them to upload high-resolution images of skin rashes,' she explained. 'Seriously, patients love it because they get to see me from their own home, and I feel like I provide more thorough care by linking to online resources than in person-to-person encounters.'

At this bamboo villa house party I found myself surrounded by fervent raw foodists, passing around portions of durian reverentially, as if it were a joint, insisting that this 'king of fruits' could get you wasted on enzymes alone. My pale skin and excess layers of clothing marked me out as a rookie, but years in Singapore had taught me to adore durian, a famously pongy fruit, so I dived in face first, gaining the immediate respect of everyone present. Visibly enjoying durian at a South East Asian party is about as macho a move as wrestling a python to the floor. Nobody messes with a white girl who likes durian.

The weed-smokers wrinkled their noses as the durian was passed around; the durian-eaters wrinkled their noses as the weed was passed around. There were a bunch of naked people in the swimming pool, but was impossible to tell if they were high on weed or durian.

If we sound like a disgraceful bunch of hedonistic expats, at least we're part of a rather grand tradition of hedonistic expats behaving disgracefully in Ubud. Bali, and Ubud specifically, has attracted writers, artists, bohemians and eccentrics since the 1920s, when the Royal Dutch Steam Packet Company added the island to its itinerary, stopping off the north coast, where passengers were ferried to shore on tenders – and the backs of brawny Balinese porters. Most would stay in the luxurious, colonial Bali Hotel in Denpasar, which opened in 1927. But then, as now, the more discriminating travellers sought out the rainforests and lush paddy fields of the interior, and the ancient princedom of Ubud. In the 1920s there was not a single hotel in Ubud; instead visitors stayed in the bamboo bungalows that Prince Tjokorda Gde Agung Sukawati had built for the circle of European artists he patronised. In 1927 the Moscow-born German painter and musician Walter Spies came to Ubud for a visit, and found a culture completely devoted to art, yet to which the notion of 'art for art's sake' was alien. The Balinese have no word for 'artist', because everybody in Bali is an artist. Carving, painting, playing the gamelan, weaving and dancing were just what you did when you weren't out in the paddy fields. Art was life. Spies was entranced, and there are countless pictures of him clad in flappy white linens, surrounded by topless Balinese beauties, to prove it.

The Ubud of the 1930s was among the most chic, bohemian destinations in the world, and Spies threw quite the dinner party. It's said that Charlie Chaplin was irked to learn that Balinese women were not as promiscuous as their bare-breasted appearance suggested, thoroughly pissed off that the nipples weren't out for his titillation alone. The radical academic and author Margaret Mead and her third husband, Gregory Bateson, got married on a steamship headed to Bali and dropped in on Spies to toast their nuptials. The actress Ruth Draper hung out being droll at dinner parties, and the heiress Barbara Hutton had a bungalow built next to Spies – briefly the subject of her ardour – but had buggered off to Persia before the bungalow was completed. H. G. Wells and Noël Coward were also guests of Spies, Coward writing a crap little ditty about Bali that doesn't really stand up to being reprinted. So even though it is human nature to deride each subsequent generation as unworthy and reckless heirs to the planet, I'm not really sure that we Hubudians were much worse than the bunch that came before.

To tell the truth, apart from the durian and the nudity, the gathering wasn't remotely debauched. After all, everyone had work to do. Turning up at Hubud the next morning felt a little like my first day at bamboo school, working out where the Fairtrade coffee was, the strategic location of standing desks that get a generous blast from the fan, the bean bags best to avoid because you're near the obnoxious Texan constantly on a conference call in the hammock.

And the moment of truth: I opened my laptop, and, yes, found that I could actually work. Remote as Hubud is, it's one of the most industrious zones on the planet. There is plenty to be nosy about. There is no music, with Indonesian lyrics or otherwise. And the sheer drive is infectious. Ambition is like a fever in Ubud, and you can smell simmering plots and plans, and frustration and opportunism in every bar and organic café.

Everyone was suspiciously friendly and helpful, until I recognised this as the island, or expat, mentality I'd experienced during my childhood in Singapore. 'In Ubud you find people who would never generally socialise together in the "real world" but necessity, and shared values, has made us a tight-knit bunch,' Hayley told me, over Jamu juice in Hubud's raw vegan café. 'You have to be when living overseas. Only recently a friend came down with dengue fever, another with typhoid, yet another in a motorbike accident. We look after one another, and use our network to cross-promote and support each other in business too.'

There's a flipside to this, of course. The line between business networking and friendship is non-existent in Hubud, as in most of the co-working spaces I've visited over the years. No conversation takes place without strings attached, people continually scanning for a way in which you can help them, or they can help you. This keenly sharpened, almost primal sense for opportunity thrills some people, but it will repulse others.

Personally, I'd rather have a little too much opportunistic fervour than too little. Being from Belfast, I always have to shout down the niggling Norn Irish voice in my head telling me to pipe down, to not trouble people, not get above my station, that pride comes before a fall. So frankly I find unfettered ambition and positivity outside a useful counterweight to what's going on inside my mind.

'When it all gets a bit much,' Hayley whispers, 'just put your headphones on, which is co-workspace code for "Do not disturb".'

And being in Bali had fringe benefits. There are yoga centres and raw vegan cafés in abundance, originally established for the *Eat, Pray, Love* brigade of thirty-something women hoping to find themselves, but now sustained by health-obsessed overachievers from So-Cal, who are equally as keen on kale as the hippies. Stressed-out start-up teams can stay in an idyllic bamboo villa sleeping six for £150 per night, adopt a 7 a.m. yoga habit at Yoga Barn across the road from Hubud, and wind down with £7 massages.

In Hubud, I soon learned that when people talk about having 'just eaten two cheeseburgers' they mean raw dehydrated burgers from the Alchemy café. When they say, 'Tao came over and we did some work' it might mean they thrashed out the business plan of their start-up, or it could mean the tantric dude came over to clear their chakras. I'd never have guessed that the high-raw, yoga-honed New Agers would have near-identical lifestyle requirements to overachieving, money-driven Silicon Valleyites, but the two worlds have synergised beautifully here in Ubud.

I slipped into my exotic new working routine with ease, doing yoga, getting hooked on jackfruit smoothies at riverside cafés and sweatily tapping away at my laptop during the day. Running my own business from something I can chuck in a rucksack is something I cherish. Over the past few years, I'd learned to ask if I could extend work press trips, booking an Airbnb or a cheap hotel for an extra few nights and working in Rome, New York or Edinburgh. Because work feels different elsewhere. I almost preferred these workaday extensions more than the frenetic sightseeing of the previous weekend. Because there's been a change in how we travel: we want to live like a local. And I realised that, dramatic as the Empire State building is, it was sitting in a café in Brooklyn with my laptop when New York really got to me. Going to a Lululemon store for yoga. It was my own regular life, but a glamorous pimped-up NYC version. It was my own life, on steroids. Swapping Netil House for Hubud for a few weeks felt like the smartest move a SAD-afflicted writer could possibly make in November.

But I'll say two things about working in paradise: firstly, you still have to work. And secondly, paradise doesn't bloody well exist so forget about it. Hubud certainly had its downsides. Mosquitos nibbling at your ankles while you take a crucial Skype call. Fingers that stick sweatily to the trackpad. A time difference that can force you into vampire-like working hours, or keep you glued to your smartphone at midnight. Hubud is twenty-four-hours a day, because many members keep strict UK or Australian office hours. For me, a 9 a.m. GMT deadline meant that I had until 3 p.m. Bali time to work on it. It also meant I was still getting work-related emails after midnight, interrupting my jackfruit vegan tacos and totally scuppering my attempt to be authentically in the moment. Some Hubudians admitted to finding themselves distracted by massages and swimming pools and jungle hikes, but I found I worked longer hours. Yes, it's perfectly possible to screw up your work–life balance in Bali, too. And I felt a lot guiltier about it here. Ultimately, I can't help feeling about nomadism the way I do about one-night stands. If something is really that good, surely you'll want to stick around and keep on doing it.

The dream that keeps digital nomads roaming is the idea that if we shift our setting, tweak our routine and steadily tinker with lifestyle upgrades, we will be better, more productive, more successful versions of ourselves. It's more than twenty years since Alex Garland's *The Beach* deftly skewered the budget backpacker scene of Thailand, sketching smug travel one-upmanship and flip-flop hedonism in a dark tale of a traveller's tireless quest for the ultimate unspoiled beach idyll – and ultimately illustrating how rapidly paradise becomes paradise lost in human hands. The quest might have changed, but the relentlessness of the pursuit has not. We're not hunting beaches now, we're hunting co-working spaces.

I've always known that travel is good for the soul, but my time in Ubud convinced me that it can also be good for my CV. It's liberating and reassuring to know that if I ever need another break from London rent or the weather, or if I felt stuck in a career rut, there's a bamboo desk waiting for me.

But, sadly, you can't leave yourself behind when you travel. And much as I relished every day in Bali as a break from my routine in Hackney, I quickly saw that there was not a wildly superior version of myself lurking behind the next palm tree. I'm stuck with what I've got. But I can occasionally take her places where she can afford a hemp smoothie.

10

Namibia: Unplugging into Adventure

In 2015, if you'd asked me what sort of travel I enjoyed the most, I'd have replied, 'all of it, thanks'. I genuinely couldn't name a single destination I wasn't interested in visiting, a single experience I would pass up. I was a glutton for travel, an insatiable brute. And then I got a job that allowed me to gorge on travel, to throw myself tits first into an orgy of trips, until I was finally ready to settle down with the trips that were right for me.

In 2015, *Stylist* magazine's deputy editor, Susan Riley, asked me if I'd be interested in the role of contributing travel editor, essentially selecting press trips, properties and destinations that were right for the magazine, organising trips by liaising with PRs, tourist boards and hotel owners, sending the right *Stylist* staffer on each trip, and finally editing the copy each week. It would be a one-day-a-week role, and I could do it from my office in Netil House in Hackney, or my sofa, or – the dream – a distant beach shack or plush hotel room. I've always felt about certain magazines the way I imagine some women feel about men; it's magazines and newspapers that make me go weak at the knees, that give me butterflies in my stomach, that make me desperately wonder if I'm pretty/cool/smart enough for them. No man has *ever* treated me as well as my job has. No man has ever flown me to Las Vegas to review pool parties. No man has ever taken me on safari to the Masai Mara. No man has ever casually introduced me to Stevie Wonder, George Clooney, Jennifer Aniston, Lena Dunham or David Attenborough, as my job did. My job thrills me on a near daily basis, my job makes me a better, more interesting and more compassionate person, my job spoils me with lovely treats like tiny bottles of shampoo and thank-you macarons at times. No man was ever going to be able to compete with my job. (No female lover would be able to, either, but frankly it's more fun to use my job to put down boyfriends than girlfriends. My girlfriends always treated me better, too. Women do.)

Stylist magazine was my Prince Charming, along with my other dishy lovers including *Grazia*, *Stella*, *Glamour*, *Cosmo*, *Women's Health*, *GQ*, *Condé Nast Traveller*, *Condé Nast Brides*, the *Daily Telegraph*, the *Guardian* and the *Sunday Times* travel section. They all treated me like a princess, a princess who deserved to be sent somewhere lovely and gifted a sarong and some dinky bottles of toiletries. After I'd returned from New Zealand, I'd worked at *Stylist* as features editor for a year, but I'd left because I realised that, much as I loved the magazine, I was a writer rather than an editor. I'd started to wonder the same thing at *Grazia* a few years before, but I am very slow and very optimistic and it took me a long time for this career realisation to finally smack me in the middle of the forehead. Now I knew that I didn't want to be the features editor sitting at a desk in the office organising an interview or amazing experience for a freelance writer. I wanted to be the first freelance writer an editor called when an opportunity came up that they couldn't take up themselves, a reliable roving reporter who knew what they needed, because I'd done that job myself in the past.

The role of contributing travel editor at *Stylist* was a dream gig for me, and I have never been able to contain my excitement about such things. 'Oh my God, really? This is the best thing ever! I want this job so much I'd pretty much do it for free!' This is how I've accepted roles at *Stylist*. And *FHM*. And, I think, *Grazia*, in between. So pretty much every job, then. It's obviously a stupid move, in terms of professional strategy, but I've never been able to contain my excitement when a magazine chose me. Me! They want me!

The role at *Stylist* also meant I could carry on writing on non-travel subjects for all my other newspapers and magazines; everything from interviewing the Californian linguist who created Dothraki for the *Independent*, reporting on smog-obliterating bicycles in China for the *Guardian*, visiting Matel HQ and being the first journalist to see a new range of Barbie dolls for *Stella*, assessing Jeremy Corbyn's fashion tastes for *Politics Today*, writing about macho musicals for *GQ* and interviewing the female diver who shot all the underwater footage for *Jaws* for the *Telegraph*. I never wanted to just be a travel writer. I want to write about cool or important stuff happening anywhere in the world. And over the years, even if I was sent to Amsterdam just to review a hotel, I'd get up early and go exploring, interrogate waiters and anyone I could find, and try to find a couple of additional stories in that destination, perhaps writing about the co-working scene there, or a crazy fitness trend, or a social dining app that was about to take over Europe. I could be in Rwanda to write about safari lodges, but I'd come home and pitch a story about how female bicycle clubs are empowering and helping rural women travel more safely. I'd visit Austin to review the Hotel Saint Cecilia, but wind up interviewing food truck owners and return to pitch a story about how food trucks allow young chefs to experiment and gain experience without the hefty overheads or financial backing needed to open a bricks-and-mortar restaurant. Press trips got me places, and my curiosity got me additional stories when I was there.

A big part of the role at *Stylist* was sending other people on trips, but, as a weekly magazine, there were a lot of trips going, and soon I was travelling a couple of times a month, away around six months of the year. It was glorious; a rolling buffet of travel that I gorged on with wanton abandon, like some sort of banquet-obliterating barbarian, leaving other, less gluttonous, travel writers behind me in my wake, rubbing their bellies and moaning about how they'd had enough of airports and they just wanted a weekend at home for once.

I've always been greedy, unable to get enough of a good thing, and irrationally bereft when I'm forced to choose between two good options, or miss something altogether. I still remember waking up with a new boyfriend, Simon, and he politely asked if I'd like tea or coffee. 'Both, thanks,' I replied as I skipped towards the shower in his shirt, blithely unaware that these were the words of a brat. But I did want both. I wanted the comforting flavour of tea. But I also needed the caffeinated jolt of coffee, if I was going to make it to work on time. 'I like a woman who knows what she wants!' he smiled, gamely. I do. And what I want is everything. It all. The lot. On a plate.

The thing about greed is that taste doesn't really come into it. That's why greed eventually needs to be reined in, tamed, or, in the case of particularly jammy bastards like me, sated. It's possible to turn a glutton into a gourmande, but it takes time and patience. And it was only after two years of virtually non-stop travel for work that I began to think about honing my tastes in travel, and wondering what I really wanted from a trip. By the end of my second year as *Stylist*'s contributing travel editor I finally accepted that I didn't need to hoard trips, panic-buy them. They weren't going to dry up. I might even, one day, say 'no' to one.

Remember when cupcake bakeries appeared and everyone went nuts for cupcakes and when they came into the office we all had to eat as many cupcakes as we could as if they were the last cupcakes on earth? Until finally we realised that cupcakes were going nowhere and that, actually, we might just prefer a scone? That. My greed made me an indiscriminate traveller, and that was unsustainable if I wanted some sort of life to return to.

One of the best things about my job was being able to Skype my dad from afar. 'Daddy! I am in Gstaad!' I would announce. 'You are in *Gstaad*,' my dad would marvel, speaking slowly and appreciatively, before telling me something important about Gstaad that I had no idea about, or quoting Thomas Mann or Voltaire or something. 'Daddy, I am in Rwanda! Daddy, I am in São Paulo! Daddy, I am in Boston!' Part of me wanted to keep on travelling, keep on collecting destinations and experiences, so I could talk about them with my dad. But I think I also dreamed about one day being able to share these experiences with children, either children or my own or nieces or nephews. Gradually, however, it struck me that the more I travelled the less I saw of these people I loved. I'd been out in the world gathering stories, but if I wasn't careful I'd soon have nobody to tell these stories to, on my return.

I was in Detroit during my friend Sali's fortieth birthday. I was in Sri Lanka for my dad's sixtieth. I missed anniversaries, concerts and so many nights out with friends that people stopped inviting me, because I seemed more likely to be away than at home. And slowly people stopped knowing the real me, and just seeing the Instagram version of my life. As we all know, objects seen though an Instagram filter appear about 60 per cent better than they really are.

On my thirty-first birthday I found myself on the National Express travelling between Gatwick and Heathrow, having returned from Sri Lanka at 10.45 p.m. and needing to check in for my morning flight to Brazil at four the next morning. So I celebrated with some overchilled M&S sushi at Gatwick and then treated myself to a mint tea at the Costa in Heathrow as I waited for the other journalists and the PR to show up. Sacrificing my birthday was worth it for Sri Lanka and Brazil, but, even so, birthdays after the age of thirty tend to be times of morose self-reflection, and sitting alone at three in the morning in that Costa, with only my rucksack to cuddle, I did wonder if I should reassess my priorities.

The trip that changed everything was a ten-day Black Tomato

tour of Namibia. When most people picture Namibia, they see the soaring red dunes of Sossusvlei; those vast, snaking, rust-coloured swirls are among the most iconic natural landscapes in the world, so iconic that they've been nicked for heaps of adverts. Namibia is *that* good. But before I even got there, the adventure began. And by 'adventure' I mean the shrieking, blind panic that ensues when a PR informs three journalists in the departures lounge that there's no Wi-Fi at any of the three safari lodges we're heading for. We spent the next forty-five minutes frantically firing off emails to editors and loved ones, explaining that we'd be off-grid for the next ten days. Like most avocado-addled millennials, I'd always imagined that the world would break should I go offline for ten days. That I'd lose friends, alienate lovers, miss out on amazing offers of work and piss off editors by not being able to respond to a query within thirty minutes. As it happened, people were thoroughly understanding, but, still, my fingers shook as I typed my out-of-office: 'Thanks for your email. I will be travelling for the next ten days with no access to the internet. I will respond to all urgent emails upon my return.' I felt as if I might as well be typing 'So long, fuckos!'

But, some thirteen hours later, I got my first glimpse of those dunes, made famous by movies as varied as *Lawrence of Arabia* and *Mad Max: Fury Road*, from a mildly terrifying six-seater Cessna transporting us from the Namibian capital, Windhoek, to Kulala Desert Lodge. Namibia is a vast, varied landscape; a country that can afford to be generous with its beauty. Sossusvlei is dune country; these soaring, snaking, seductive sand dunes are probably Namibia's most famous landmark. That first day, we climbed the pervily named 'Big Daddy', the tallest of the bunch at 325 metres, scaling his spine, before running down the forty-five-degree incline, kicking sand as we went, reaching the bottom in under a minute. (It takes ninety sweaty minutes to get to the top.) In late afternoon we roared off on quad bikes, streaking through the wilderness reserve, spotting springbok, oryx and birds of prey, before returning to camp, happy and exhausted, for sundowners and a game barbecue on the deck.

In Namibia, even going to bed can be an adventure; Sossusvlei is remarkably predator-free, a rarity in Africa, so I tried to banish all thoughts of being eaten by a lion or nibbled by mosquitos and sleep in the open air on a mattress on my rooftop deck, with nothing between my nose and the Milky Way. To be honest, it took me a while to talk myself into this. Sleeping under the stars is different when you're honeymooners, or couple of gung-ho grey-gappers in their sixties. Safaris aren't really a solo pursuit, partly because they're so bloody expensive. And so I found myself wondering if any other solo female traveller had ever chosen to sleep outdoors on the roof of her desert bungalow. But Namibia is one of the best stargazing destinations on the planet, a desert sky with virtually no light pollution, and this felt like an opportunity I couldn't miss. So I whipped out my usual mantra: 'You will get up there on the roof and go to sleep, Anna, because you are an adventurous badass and IT IS YOUR JOB.' And, within minutes, I couldn't have felt more relaxed, all thoughts of predators, animal or human, having evaporated. Five minutes of stargazing has got to be the head-clearing equivalent of a good forty-five-minute meditation session on Headspace, or an hour-long massage. I drifted off to sleep with a peaceful mind cleared of everything but stars.

But it wasn't just the sky at night that was clearing my mind. It was the absence of my phone. After just two days I was feeling the benefits. I no longer had that twitchy feeling that I should be checking something every five minutes. And removed from the stream of work-related emails, Instagram angst and the pulse-quickening offers of press trips, I began to think about why this trip felt so special, and why others had left me oddly untouched, just a little bit fatter, hungover and tired. Perfectly nice trips to new spa hotels in Provence, openings of new hotel restaurants in Tuscany, wine-tasting in Portugal: all of these sound like lovely, lovely things to do – but the sort of things I'd like to do on my own terms, with someone I'm shagging or my funniest friend.

TECHNOLOGY AND TRAVEL: HOW TO GET IT RIGHT

Embrace Flight Mode. I flick my iPhone on to flight mode (aka fuck-off-mode) for chunks of the day, rendering this so-called smartphone blissfully stupid. The camera and clock still works, but this extra barrier on data stops me twitchily checking my phone every few minutes.

Do make Instagram work for you, not the other way around. Ignore social media snobs; it's entirely possible to stay connected on holiday without spoiling a single sunset.

The trick is to not Instagram in real time. I keep my phone offline for as much of the day as I can, then do a swift Instagram edit/caption session when I'm back at the hotel room. I also get sneaky and queue my posts manually by uploading them whilst on flight mode. This means I still get to share my amazing travel experiences, without interrupting that experience to fiddle with filters.

Don't feel guilty about picking up your laptop. Today our jobs are part of our personality, and so the idea that we must unceremoniously abandon this facet of ourselves when we go on holiday has always struck me as a little bit perverse. We're told that if we don't fastidiously suppress any mention of work, switch off all our devices, and push our professions into the furthermost corners of our minds, we're not *really* on holiday; that all travel is automatically compromised when we mix business and pleasure. In my experience, a trip away can prove a much-needed catalyst for career development. A change of scene can give us the headspace we need to think about the future. We've always travelled for one principal reason: we want to return transformed in some way. We don't travel simply to explore new destinations; we also want to explore new corners of our character, challenge ourselves and embark upon an emotional journey as well as a physical one. Why would we take career transformations off the menu?

But consider going long-hand. As a writer I can't imagine going away without my laptop; however, I've recently discovered the joy of writing in notebooks, then typing up articles, diary entries or fragments of books later. For a start, this means less time at a screen, and it means you can scribble outside where it feels like a treat, rather than work. And I firmly believe that something magical happens when we put pen to paper, and we wind up being more creative. I scribbled every chapter of this book in a notebook, from far-flung corners of the globe, or down by the sea in Margate with a little flask of wine. Scribbling rather than typing made writing feel like a luxury, rather than a task.

An older, wiser journalist once said to me, 'Never mistake a press trip for a holiday.' She was right. A press trip can be amazing, but they are never relaxing. I've been invited for two-night trips to Cape Town, making the travel time:trip ratio an unfavourable 2:1. I've been on ridiculous itineraries in Las Vegas where we had half-hourly appointments at different hotels and restaurants from 7 a.m. until 11 p.m. each night. I've moved on from a beautiful clifftop lodge in Dominica after just fifteen hours there, realising that I'd never had a moment to step into the outdoor shower, let alone relax in the private infinity pool or even sit on one of the loungers. Press trips never feel like anything but work. Travel is still a job, even if it's the best job in the world.

In some ways I loved the school trip element of press trips, whereby a selection of PR-approved journalists writing for hotel/destination-approved newspapers or magazines meet at the departure gate for the first time, and say a sleepy hello to their twenty-four-hour travel companions for the next weekend/

week/month. I have met amazing journalists this way: grizzled old war correspondents from the *Daily Mail*, experienced TV travel presenters like Sarah Siese, adorable and glamorous fashion bloggers like my friend Emily Johnston of Fashion Foie Gras, and hilarious, adventurous boys like Jonathan Thompson, Jack Dyson and Damien Gabet. But a weekend at a hotel in Ravello? You want that trip to be with someone you're fucking.

Talking of fucking people, I met a lot of fucking idiot tourists on safari, which is exactly where you don't want to meet an idiot. Our next stop in Namibia was Desert Rhino Conservation Camp, set among the rolling, rocky hills of the Palmwag Concession, home to the largest free-roaming black rhino population in Africa. And we went rhino-tracking, on foot, with rangers, from the Save the Rhino Trust, who don't carry stun guns. Which is obviously a good thing, for the rhinos. But we were also going rhino-tracking with some idiots, which was less of a good thing for us humans. Rhinos are among the rarest, and grumpiest, animals on the planet, and getting within a hundred metres of a mother and calf was a thrill made only more potent by an American tourist's phone going off at a critical moment. And he *answered it*. We were told that if a rhino charged, one of the rangers would throw a rock to one side to distract it, which gave the entire caper a cartoon-like quality. A scary, dangerous kind of cartoon; but the rhinos chose to shrug off that particular bit of idiocy. And the taste of danger in our mouths only made my whisky and soda at sunset taste all the more delicious.

The next day we moved towards the coast at Hoanib Camp,

where we careered up a dried-up riverbed in search of elephants at sunset. We scaled a rocky outcrop where we could
safely watch a herd of fifteen elephants grazing, and wound up
spending a couple of unscheduled – but happy – hours there
while an elephant in musth circled the hill, blocking our exit
route. We silently inched the final thirty metres to the safety of
our Land Rover, then sped down the riverbed back to camp.
Adventure had become an everyday occurrence in Namibia
and I loved it. My days felt worthwhile. And I remembered
that, years ago, it was adventure travel that got me going. It
was active, intrepid trips I spent my hard-earned cash on. And
the trips that stand out in my mind from recent years – diving
in Belize, cross-country skiing in the Dolomites, kite-surfing in
Mauritius, hiking in New Zealand – they all fall into the cate-
gory of adventure travel.

The trips I can hardly remember are those to spa hotels in
Austria or Italy. Full disclosure: I am a spa snob. I don't mean
that I demand to be transported from jacuzzi to sauna in a fluffy
cotton sedan chair, or massaged with kid gloves. I mean that I
don't really enjoy them, unless they are badass Swiss or German
medi-spas with serious clinical chops. This past decade, however, I've watched the word 'spa' pop up all over the place, in
places it patently does not belong. Today every three-star motor
lodge claims to have a 'health spa', when what they really have
is 'a battered treadmill and a bored manicurist'. I am distinctly
suspicious of the s-word. The word 'pampering' is to me one
of the most odious in the English language, and I find forced
relaxation even more enraging than forced fun. The one-size-
fits-all approach to luxury at spa hotels depresses me; I resent

the assumption that my idea of a treat is an oversized bathrobe and a TV in the shower, and panpipes music, perhaps a glass of prosecco for the laydees. 'You don't know me, you dickhead of a spa!' I want to shriek, kicking the mosaic-tiled wall of the Balinese-inspired hammam with my sodden white slipper. 'I don't want ostentatious service, uniform interiors, a frosty layer of formality and absurd flourishes like gargantuan flat-screen TVs. I don't want your stupid tinkly spa music, I don't want to lie for fifteen minutes sipping stupid cold tea after my stupid half-assed massage, and I don't want to spend £150 on products recommended for my skin type by someone working for commission.'

Happily, the world of women's magazines is not short of exhausted editors who are desperate for a spa weekend, who don't get twitchy on a sun lounger after ten minutes, who don't dread a massage in case it tickles them too much. So I could leave those trips to them, and go and get my hands dirty up a mountain.

My early career was shaped by everything I said yes to – which was pretty much every offer, every opportunity, every commission that landed in my inbox. But if your career in your twenties is determined by what you say yes to, your career in your thirties is determined by what you say no to. It's the offers, the jobs, the positions you turn down that shape your career because this is the only way to clear space for new opportunities and progress. Saying yes to everything is important at the start, as you gain experience and prove yourself to be keen and reliable. But by your thirties you're demonstrably good at what you do, and saying yes to the same old stuff starts holding you back.

The flattery of being wanted for a job, or the repeat satisfaction of nailing it, as you always do, shouldn't be enough to make you say yes when you want to move on. You only make progress by turning down the stuff you can do blindfolded, or the jobs you got bored of doing five years ago.

I realised that I had to adopt a similar mindset with regard to how I travelled. I could carry on reviewing swish spa hotels in the Lake District, or I could turn this offer down, politely explain to editors that I specialise in adventure/active travel and unusual city destinations, cringe after hitting 'send' on that email, use Netflix/running/yoga/sex as a distraction technique and then wait for the right commission to come my way. Basically, I needed to be more of a diva, and less of an eager-to-please yes-girl. I needed to be more Grace Jones about travel.

Most women need to be a bit more Grace Jones about everything. We aren't that great at saying no to stuff, or saying that we think something is crap. But I've got a lot better at saying no, and I've learned to be upfront about my likes and dislikes. This has been interesting, because I actively dislike a lot of things that seemingly everybody else likes: *The Shawshank Redemption* (irredeemably mawkish and worthy chick-flick beloved by men who are unable to express emotion in any other way); barbecues (having no control over your mealtime makes me panicky, plus the food is simultaneously burned and raw); wind (stop BLOWING me, you vindictive element); amateur stand-up comedy (like being on the worst Tinder date ever); Daft Punk (electronic music for people who don't like electronic music and would rather be listening to Ed Sheeran).

And, you know, it's been FUN getting in touch with my inner grumpy bastard. The side of me that is less easily pleased. The side that knows what she wants, and, sorry, that's not you, you loser. Today, if someone offers me a tea or a coffee, I no longer need to ask for both. I drink supercharged Matcha tea that delivers the delicate flavour of green tea with a powerful caffeine kick that gets me from my bed to my laptop in six minutes. By your thirties, you know what works for you and what doesn't.

Namibia, of course, made it easy to dreamily envisage my idyllic future as an adventure travel specialist. This was a blissfully spa-free zone, and I was in my element. I felt like the travel writer I'd always wanted to be – gung-ho, positive, active and up for every challenge. We wound up our ten-day trip in one of the most desolate spots I've ever seen, the Skeleton Coast, so-called because of the numerous shipwrecks that lace this vast stretch of the Atlantic coastline, and also because of the animal skulls – elephant, oryx, springbok, even lion – that used to be washed here by rivers that have now been dry for decades. We slithered down dunes on our bums, on sand where there was no need for sledges. We visited the eerie shipwreck museum at the ranger's station, full of formaldehyde snakes, whale and elephant skulls, shipwreck relics and maudlin, yellowed newspaper clippings about seafaring tragedies. It was like the ultimate Tinder date for emos. (Yes, this is my dream Tinder date.)

Flying home from Windhoek, I felt none of the normal travel fatigue I'd get from a weekend in Europe. I was delivered back to my day job as a writer in London with my priorities reshuffled back into the correct order, with a smile on my face, into a world that seemed full of promise again. Adventures *work*, I realised. Adventures, and activity, and mind-blowing beauty: that's what I travel for. That's what makes me tick. This was the sort of travel I needed to settle down to, forsaking all others. I promised myself that I'd no longer run away for dirty weekends with spa hotels that meant nothing to me. I'd travel less, but I'd travel smarter. I'd travel like Grace Jones. My three years as a globe-trotting travel editor had taught me what sort of traveller I wanted to be. I'd tried it all, and I was returning to my first love: adventure.

11

Singapore: Going Back to My Roots

Within traveller circles Singapore has long suffered by comparison to other South East Asian cities. Backpacking around Thailand in my twenties, I regularly heard Singapore dismissed as 'sterile' or 'boring', lacking the hedonistic chaos of Bangkok, the cultural clout of Hanoi, the frenetic energy of Phnom Penh. *Real* travellers preferred these cities, I was smugly told. I had zero patience for such views, which I've always believed say much more about the traveller than the destination. A lot of long-term travellers, let's face it, are twats.

In 1990, I stood in the city's National Stadium, holding hands with my six-year-old sister, Naomi, and my four-year-old brother, Peter, as fireworks exploded to mark the nation state's twenty-fifth birthday. Singapore's list of achievements by this tender age was remarkable, but all that the grown-ups could talk about, in worried terms, what the next two decades could possibly hold for this economic starlet, the poster child for Asian financial growth.

Because, even as a child, I understood that the general consensus was that Singapore's rapid financial advancement had been purchased at too high a cost: culture. A British colony from 1819 until the Second World War, Singapore gained independence from Malaysia in 1965. The new nation state's first prime minister, the venerable Lee Kuan Yew, promised to quell racial tensions, provide public housing, eradicate corruption and promote rapid economic growth. Lee Kuan Yew's draconian methods (journalists and political opponents were routinely sued and silenced) are still hotly debated, but when he passed away aged ninety-one in March 2015, Singaporeans turned out in their droves to mourn the statesman who steered them from poverty and political unrest into the economic success story of South East Asia.

Most Singaporeans that we knew considered the government overly authoritarian, but any criticism was tempered by a sense of national pride; in fact, *relief* that their young nation state was alive and kicking, that it hadn't floundered economically, or descended into racial chaos like Sri Lanka. Today, Singapore is one of Asia's most ethnically diverse and racially integrated cities, with significant Malay, Indian and Eurasian minorities alongside the 74 per cent Chinese Singaporean majority. Five decades ago Lee Kwan Yew granted the languages of all four major ethnic groups – Malay, Tamil, Mandarin and English – equal status, but in practice English became the primary language of Singapore. For expatriates and international travellers, the absence of a language barrier made it easy to connect with Singaporeans, and their kindness, generosity and openness, surely the legacy of a (relatively) class-free melting pot of cultural influences, made a family of Irish expats feel welcome.

The city was an unmitigated economic success story, but neighbouring Asian capitals regarded their precocious little sister with suspicion, jealousy and a touch of derision, while international visitors dismissed Singapore as an English-speaking, litter-free, curiously Scandinavian outpost in the heart of South East Asia.

But for our first few years in Singapore I was happy, finding lots to love about my adopted city (even in 1992, when the new prime minister, Goh Chok Tong, banned chewing gum and we returned from a family holiday in Melaka to the devastating news that Hubba Bubba would never again grace Singaporean shop shelves). Singaporeans joked that they live in a 'fine city: you're fined for littering, for smoking, for carrying a durian on the MRT'.

Singapore's crazed commitment to total excellence and superlatives meant we could visit the world's best zoo, fly out of the world's best airport, scale the world's tallest building and stroll the world's cleanest streets. The wild abandon with which Singaporeans view mealtimes is by turns exhilarating and exhausting; if a friend offered to take us to '*the* best restaurant', it might be a hawker centre selling $5 bowls of chicken rice or a gourmet affair in a five-star hotel. My mum never knew what to wear out to dinner, but we rapidly became adventurous eaters.

Our Singaporean friends also introduced us to a deliciously un-British brand of hospitality. In Britain, hospitality means a bed, a biscuit and possibly a beer; we'd never dare imagine that a visitor wants to be dragged around our crummy old town. In

Singapore, a young, enthusiastic and proud nation, hospitality means pulling strings to get us family membership at a local sports club, inviting us along to ten-course wedding banquets, treating us to buffet brunches at the Mandarin Oriental or Westin Stamford, and generally introducing us to all the delights that Singapore's petite dimensions contain. I plainly absorbed all this, and today I feel a distinctly Singaporean fervour when someone comes to visit, a feverish desire to unveil my environs with a showman's flourish: Tah-DAH! An overpriced Scandinavian café! WITNESS the ducks on this manmade pond! HURRY or we'll miss happy hour at the pub and be unable to afford a beer. It must be exhausting, visiting me. This is something I get from Singapore.

As Singapore prepared to celebrate its Golden Jubilee in 2015, I decided to plot a return visit, and worked with Singapore Tourism Board to set up a couple of commissions for *Stylist* magazine, *Travel Weekly* and *Business Traveller*. In a major professional and personal coup, Singapore Tourism also paid for flights for my sister, a photographer, so that she could document our trip. Normally with press trips I'm flying solo, or in a group of other random journalists, who gather at the gate, say our hellos, and then try not to fight or drunkenly shag each other over the next few days. Travelling with my beloved little sister, Naomi, who was my chief companion when I was in Singapore first time around, felt like a true gift. I flew in from London and hopped around on one foot with excitement while I waited for Naomi to arrive from LA. We met in the gleaming arrivals hall of Changi Airport, an airport so swish – butterfly grottos, rooftop pools, twenty-seven-metre waterfalls – that we used to come here on family days out. To be honest, there was part of me that was seriously nervous about the trip ahead. I knew that it would be more emotionally challenging than my average press trip. I'm used to physically challenging trips – sleeping solo under the desert skies of Namibia, scaling peaks, lengthy cross-country bike rides – but I wasn't sure how I'd handle a tidal wave of childhood memories, and a mixed bag of memories at that. Naomi was there partly as my photographer, but she was also there to prop me up.

FOUR WAYS TO GET UNDER THE SKIN OF A DESTINATION

Visit a local beauty salon or barbers. I never understand the desperation to get a pedicure before a holiday, when visiting a local salon in your destination town is usually a) cheaper, and b) such a fun cultural experience.

Give blood. Many hospitals are woefully short of blood, and, for travellers, donating blood and visiting a local hospital opens a fascinating window into the everyday tragedies and triumphs of life here, sweeping aside the chintzy curtains hastily strung up to separate tourists from reality. I'd urge you all to consider it. Plus you normally get a free Coke or a biscuit.

Bring a skill. Perhaps you can code, arrange flowers, tell people how to promote their business through social

media, arrange a window in a charity shop, talk about permacul-
ture or make *kombucha*. There might be a school, a social club,
a co-working space or a cafe that needs speakers, tutors or vol-
unteers. Think about what you can bring to the party, because
contributing to the local community is the very best way to plug
yourself into a new place.

Or just bring the right stuff. Websites like stuffyourrucksack
lists items needed in specific destinations, so you can donate
school supplies and other essentials to the far-flung places that
need them most.

Everyone is familiar with Singapore's skyline, because it's
pretty much a standard-issue Asian city skyline, similar to Hong
Kong, Bangkok or Kuala Lumpur. Most visitors stay in the
skyscraper hotels of the CBD, but I like my hotels how I don't
like my jeans: low-rise. And given how easily navigable the city
is via the MRT network, and greedy to take in as many of our
old 'hoods as possible, we split our nights between two boutique
hotels in historic quarters, the New Majestic in Chinatown, and
its sister hotel, Wanderlust, in Little India. Minutes from the
New Majestic is the newly pedestrianised Food Street, where we
joined the lunchtime hoards to feast on satay and fried *hokkien
mee* (Singapore's answer to pad thai) while admiring the elegant,
colourful, crumbling shopfront facades. Today I can appreciate
the weird convenience of speaking English to Singaporean
stallholders and diners. For the culturally curious traveller,

no language barrier allows you to get under Singapore's skin swiftly. For the greedy traveller, it allows you to order what you want to eat from every stall. And food is a national obsession here, the main flavour of idle chitchat: Singaporeans bond over their favourite hawker centres the way the British talk about the weather. There is relatively little status in wearing a designer label in Singapore, but knowing the best place to get chicken rice? That's a true sign of character. In acknowledgement of this, the 2016 *Michelin Guide* awarded a Singaporean chicken rice stallholder, Liao Fan, a star for his £1.50 dish. Food is a gloriously democratic pleasure in Singapore, and every single meal is an opportunity.

As Naomi and I wandered around the city that we'd called home for so long, we were floored by what was new. Today, Singapore has lost none of its zeal for modernisation – but Singapore's definition of progress has evolved dramatically. Now, at the grand old age of fifty, Singapore has definitely rediscovered its cultural heritage and creative bent. If Sydney has its Opera House, Singapore now has the Esplanade – Theatres on the Bay, 60,000 square metres of beautifully designed performing arts space including a concert hall seating about 1,800 and a 2,000-capacity theatre that was gearing up for the blockbuster Christmas ballet *The Nutcracker*. Meanwhile, the theatres at Marina Bay Sands are drawing Broadway and West End hits such as *The Phantom of the Opera*, *Wicked* and *Les Miserables*. We would have loved this shit when we were kids.

Meanwhile, within the visual arts, in the past five years Singapore has cemented its reputation as an international art hub, something that would have been unthinkable in the 1990s. 2011 saw the opening of the much-lauded ArtScience Museum, a lotus-flower-shaped building uniting art and science exhibitions. Singapore is always in hot pursuit of superlatives; accordingly, no architectural blueprint is too trippy, no cultural concept too wanky. Just as exciting is Gillman Barracks, a former 1930s British military encampment, now converted into the island's newest centre for contemporary art, consisting of museums, commercial galleries, non-profit spaces and venue space for major art events such as the Singapore Biennale and Art Stage Singapore. And in 2015 National Gallery Singapore in the Downtown Core arrived on the scene, with the world's largest public collection of Singaporean and South East Asian art, totalling more than 8,000 artworks. I lose interest after about fifty of them, but I can appreciate the effort.

Happily, Singapore hasn't lost her penchant for showy leisure flourishes, and today the multi-award-winning Zoological Gardens have been usurped by the multi-award-winning Botanical Gardens at Marina Bay, but the British landscaping firm was selected for their eco-mindedness and creativity rather than sheer scale and grandiosity. By nature Singaporeans are culturally curious, creatively inclined and collectively supportive of talent and innovation, and accordingly Singapore has a thriving arts scene that spans outdoor concerts and Broadway shows to homegrown musical talent and edgy public art.

Perhaps even more interesting to us is how hip Singapore has become. I have a problem with the label 'hipster', which seems to me a pretty lazy way of disparaging young people who like nice things. But it's hard not to hear it ringing in my ears as we wandered around Kampong Glam, the Arab quarter, finding independent boutiques with names like Threadbare and Squirrel alongside retro barber shops and – the ultimate badge of hipster pride – a Tokyobike store, positioning Singapore alongside Copenhagen, Berlin, Melbourne and London's Shoreditch. Tiong Bahru, a 1930s housing estate that US *Vogue* recently named one of the world's hippest neighbourhoods, is all quirky bookstores, record stores and buzzy cafés. Sipping flat whites and admiring the barista's vintage dress, we agreed that Singapore is a city we'd happily live in for another seven years, today. Because if the first twenty-five years were about building skyscrapers, in this decade Singapore is all about what's happening at street level.

Much as Naomi and I were full of admiration for Singapore's reinvention, we were perhaps affected more by what had stayed spookily the same, the jolts of recognition that kept us on our toes as we explored. The entire city was tinged with nostalgia for us; we never knew when the smell of a familiar soap or a billboard advertising our old brand of toothpaste would take us back to 1992.

I've never really known quite what to *do* with nostalgia. As a society we've seemingly embraced the feel-good factor of nostalgia (everyone owns something with that bloody 'Keep Calm and Carry On' slogan on it) but it wasn't always couched in such positive terms. The word derives from the Greek 'nostos' (return) and 'algos' (pain), describing a suffering borne out of the desire to return to one's place of origin. The word 'nostalgia' dates back to the 1688 dissertation of a Swiss doctor called Johannes

Hofer, who coined the term to describe anxieties displayed by Swiss mercenaries fighting in the lowlands of France and Italy. (Some military doctors believed this ailment to be specific to the Swiss nation and in some way related to the sound of cowbells.) By the 1850s nostalgia was no longer considered a disease, and was instead understood to be a form of melancholia and a predisposing condition among suicides. And sometimes, well, I think these Swiss doctors weren't entirely wrong. Nostalgia isn't as simple as fondly remembering the past. In me, anyway, it's tainted by a melancholic sense that I can never return to that place. Nostalgia and I have a very complex relationship. I will never buy one of those Keep Calm tea towels.

Plenty of my memories of Singapore are happy, but I've never trusted anyone who claims to have enjoyed a blissfully happy childhood. Show me someone who says, 'Best days of my life, my school years! I excelled at sports and was well-liked in my year. Always felt pretty sure of myself around teachers, too', and I'll show you a fucking sociopath who is destined for an adulthood of simmering resentment, sexual dysfunction and frustrated ambition. All the most successful people I know today were the misfits at school, the shy, awkward or troublesome kids who spent their strange childhoods dreaming of a happy adult existence and working out how to get it.

I was a strange, painfully sensitive and overly sentimental kid, and Singapore is where I became myself. Naomi and I decided to give nostalgia a go, though, and veered off the wonderful itinerary prepared for us by Singapore Tourism, and headed for Holland Village, now a hellish expat drinking den, which was *the* shopping centre to hang out at when we were kids. This is where we spent long, happy hours flicking through second-hand copies of *Sweet Valley High* books and Archie comics in the bookstore on the top floor.

Naomi and I made a little pilgrimage to that very store. But as we walked around the gift and furniture shops, the scent of a jasmine air freshener took me back to my secondary school, UWC, and specifically to the head of year's office. And suddenly, I am twelve years old again, in her office, explaining awkwardly about a boy in the year above cornering me in the girls' toilets after my clarinet lesson, how strange I'd found it at first, how he'd told me he'd killed girls before and he'd kill me, too, how I didn't understand why he wanted to put his arms around my chest, and how sick I'd felt before I hit him with my clarinet case and ran away, breaking free of his tight grip around my wrist, which left me with bruises. I remembered how I'd had to break it to my mother, by slinking into her room as she got ready for bed and toying with her earrings on her dresser, until I finally said, 'Mummy, something yucky happened to me at school today.' And with my adult eyes, I can see how heartbreaking that scene was, how enraged and devastated my mother must have been underneath her calm, caring expression. With my adult mind I feel grateful for the female head teacher, who acted immediately and unequivocally and expelled the boy who attacked me. And with a grown-up soul, I think of all the other girls and women who experience sexual attack or abuse, by which I mean just about every one of us, and I wonder if we all get to tell a loving mother, and have it dealt with swiftly by an understanding woman in authority. And I wonder how it affected me, even so, and how such things affect us all.

Revisiting a destination from your past shakes up all sorts of feelings, and I felt probed in parts of my psyche that had lain dormant for years. I wasn't just affected by the changes in Singapore, I realised, but by the changes in me.

As we drove past Changi Prison, I remember when my grandparents, who are now both dead and desperately missed, came to visit us, and my grandpa went to Changi, a place where many of his friends had been imprisoned, coming home oddly quiet and unable to return the boisterous hugs of three small grandchildren. He told me the most horrific story about the war, about how his friend Jock, 'a lovely, big sandy-haired fellow', had been shot down in Japanese-occupied Burma, and when they found him he'd been strung up between two trees and smothered in sugar syrup, so that the ants would eat him alive. 'Was he okay?' I asked, with all the idiotic optimism of a nine-year-old who watched too many movies. 'He was still breathing, but he was gone, he was out of his wits by then,' said Grandpa, and he got up from his rattan chair and went out on to the balcony.

As we drove past the hospital my mum had worked at, Singapore University Hospital, I remembered running around those corridors as if I owned the place. I've always been comfortable in hospitals, because, to me, they are the place where my mum worked, my own playground. I remembered Mum rushing home every evening to our flat in Katong, just in time for tea, looking glamorous in her late 1980s earrings and her permed hair, and thinking how I hoped that one day I'd have a job that would make my children proud. I wanted to come home from my important job just in time for tea at 6.30 p.m., with dangly earrings and a bag stuffed with papers, and a big smile for my kids. That was motherhood to me. And I wondered if I've ever let my mum know this: how cool I thought she was.

Memories are renegade thoughts to me; I have no control over them whatsoever, and don't know how to tame them when they ride roughshod into my frontal lobe. And so perhaps it's no accident that we saved our visit to Joo Chiat until the very last day. Singapore Tourism had kindly organised a dumpling-making masterclass at the historic Kim Choo shophouse. And these dumplings – Nyonya *bak chang* – happened to be our favourite dish on the planet. When we were growing up, we loved Joo Chiat, but it was unquestionably rough around the edges, bordering the red-light district, and none of our friends at the international schools across town would have dreamt of going there.

Today, Joo Chiat is the best place to discover living and breathing Peranakan culture. Peranakan culture in Singapore stems from the intermarriage of Chinese immigrants and local Malays, dating back to the seventeenth century onwards. As bilingual and culturally progressive merchants and traders, Peranakan culture is rich and distinctive, and the colourful two-storey shophouses, crumbling terraced homes and scent of dumplings and *laksa* makes Joo Chiat one of the most charming heritage quarters of Singapore. Today independent boutiques and hip chalkboard-and-Wi-Fi cafés sit next to traditional eating houses spooning out *laksa* and *kueh chang* alongside other Nyonya delicacies. My dad was the minister just around the corner, at Katong Presbyterian Church, for seven years, and Naomi and I spent our formative years running around these streets, eating these dumplings, marvelling at these crumbling shophouses, which I thought looked like wedding cakes.

At the Kim Choo shophouse, the young proprietor, Edmond Wong, spoke proudly of the Peranakan culture of the early Chinese settlers to Singapore; he runs educational programmes in schools, heritage walking tours and is currently transforming the family shophouse into a mini-museum. Two decades ago, Singaporeans spoke of culture and the arts in apologetic tones, painfully aware that much had been lost in the race to prosperity. Today this lack of confidence is long gone, and young Singaporeans seem aware that they all have a part to play in their city's cultural resurgence. Edmond disappeared for a few moments, and then came back with a wide grin on his face. 'It's the strangest thing, but I remember an Irish pastor at my church around the corner, and his three children. The Harts.' Suddenly, I remembered Edmond, playing with my brother Peter in the garden of the manse at the church. We spoke fondly of the families we used to know: the Gohs, the Leongs, the Tans. And I realised that, for me, the real pain of nostalgia isn't about wanting to return to the past. At its most pointed, my nostalgia is a form of guilt. Guilt for being too shy or too strange to show how much I appreciated the kindness of our Singaporean friends, or the love of my parents and siblings, or the generosity of my school friends. But it's also tinged with sympathy for my younger self, or a new, adult understanding of a place, person or scenario. It's a wish to return to the past, with eyes that have been bathed in adulthood, to tell people how grateful I am for them, how I understand now why they did what they did. I suppose, in its essence, nostalgia is about belated gratitude, an adult appreciation for what I had, and how it made me who I am today.

I know that my seven years in Singapore opened my eyes to the wider world outside, and what happens to a human being when we're introduced to a radically new environment, forced to charm a whole new group of people and exposed to new sensations. In Singapore, I realised early on that I am at my best in the role of outsider, when I can't rely lazily on the unconditional love and support of friends and family, or the comfort of the familiar. Growing up between Belfast and Singapore taught me, at a very young age, that travel offers us the endless opportunity to reinvent ourselves. Maybe this spirit of reinvention, of the past being something that has to be processed into a positive future, is the most valuable thing I've learned from this spirited and big-hearted city.

And modern-day Singapore feels like an appropriate place to ponder all this, because Singapore now wears her past on her sleeve; the Singaporean culture and art of the future is a dialogue with Singapore's colourful but often painful history. Singapore has always been good at surprises, a mistress of reinvention, but even I couldn't have predicted that Singapore at the age of fifty would be more creative, relaxed, fun and cultured than the twenty-five-year-old I knew and loved. At the grand old age of fifty, Singapore has finally gained her confidence, and discovered her playful side. Perhaps there is hope for me yet.

12

LA: The LA/London Life Swap

Sometimes a holiday is not enough for a destination that steals your heart. A good trip can resemble a heady but cruelly short fling. After one such love affair – perhaps Naples, or Detroit, or Zadar – I found myself curled up morosely on my sofa in Hackney, glass of red wine in hand, The Smiths in my ears, frustrated longing in my heart. I wondered if by becoming a travel writer I'd foolishly chosen a career which doomed me to constant heartbreak. Because I leave virtually every place I visit lusting for more, swearing I'll return soon, incapable of truly saying goodbye. I've flirted with a life in Zadar, you see, and, like every good flirt, I give a little bit too much of my heart away in the exchange.

Some of these travel flings were secret affairs, unfolding surreptitiously on group press trips, when I'd board the flight home with other journalists who seemed oddly untouched by their brief encounter with Pienza, or Chicago, or Galle. I'd gaze around at their placid faces as they emailed friends and family and irate editors back home, and sink back into my seat with a secret smile. Because I knew that me and Chicago, we had a thing going on. Chicago felt differently about me than it felt about the other journalists; I was special.

And unfortunately for my long-suffering soul, there are few places I've been where I haven't felt that chemistry, where I haven't been able to fantasise giddily about a happy life there. I am outrageously good at fantasy. Leaving New Zealand was a wrench, because I'd seen the beach house I wanted to live in, visited the farmers' market I'd be at every Sunday, even mentally purchased the surfboard I'd chuck on top of my mentally purchased VW campervan every morning. Leaving my grown-up, newly rediscovered Singapore hurt like hell, because I knew I could happily set up home in Katong and continue my voyage of rediscovery. Bali, too, I could have stayed in for so, so much longer – my month there left me with friends I'll keep forever.

But I would take my new life fantasies even further, into dangerous terrain. I would bolster my fantasy about a life in Chicago with some practical observations, perhaps checking out the rental prices for one-bedroom flats in Ukrainian Village. This is a bad move, trust me, because when you introduce a flicker of reality into a giddy fantasy that is when fantasy gets dangerous. That is when fantasy becomes mobilised.

There was one particular place in the world I'd avoided on group press trips, because I suspected, deep in my heart, that a weekend or even a two-week fling wouldn't be nearly enough. I knew enough about this destination to understand that it would be a passionate love affair, a romance I'd never be able to get out of my system in a few short weeks.

California and I, we needed months together, because I've been quietly obsessing over her – through films, music and books – all my life. Paris, London, Rome, New York and Kyoto are cities that are heavy with cultural significance, but pop cultural significance? Los Angeles wins. And I am poppy, through and through.

California had seeped into my ears through the songs of The Beach Boys, The Doors, Fleetwood Mac, Frank Zappa and Captain Beefheart, 1960s and 70s rock music that I'd discovered as a creepily culturally precocious teenager. I guess I had to be precocious in some way, and I was a seriously late starter on all other counts; I was years behind the other girls at school in the fields of periods, make-up, first kisses, smoking, drinking, style and Stephen King movies. I guess I tested my nascent adolescent confidence through popular culture. I was listening to Beefheart's *Safe As Milk* when I was still too cripplingly shy to phone for a pizza.

California sank into my eyes as I watched films like Hitchcock's *Vertigo*, David Lynch's *Mulholland Drive*, and, um, *Pretty Woman* and *Beverly Hills Cop*. I know that *Beverly Hills Cop* might not be up there with Beefheart in terms of cultural credentials, but Axel Foley has a special place in my heart.

And reading books like Jack Kerouac's *On the Road* (yawn, but it looked good on my bookshelf), Armistead Maupin's *Tales of the City* (a breathless love letter to San Francisco) and everything ever by John Steinbeck (glorious, every single volume) made my fantasies about California 3D.

Few destinations summon as many daydreams as California, famed throughout the last century for delivering *la dolce vita*, New

World-style. And so one damp September, when Sean didn't get a job after finishing horticultural college, as he'd hoped and expected, I decided not to see this as a major bummer, but as an opportunity to escape London, to have a grown-up gap year – or at least a few months in the sunshine. So Sean took an internship at LA's Huntington Gardens in Pasadena (equally beloved by wealthy old women and CalArts students on LSD) and I sorted out a media visa enabling me to write for UK publications for a few months.

There was another reason for this London/LA life swap: my beloved sister Naomi was living the dream of many an Irish girl and had married a Californian surfer called Brandon, and they lived together in Topanga Canyon. Naomi and Brandon were having a baby in January, and I wanted to be there for this momentous occasion. I was beyond excited about being an overprotective, adoring big sister to Naomi, and an overbearing, eccentric auntie to her son. Eccentric auntie is the role I was born for.

I began plotting and planning. We could afford to take a couple of weeks off at the start of November, to charge around California before settling down to work in LA. I considered trying to review hotels the whole way up the Pacific Coast Highway, but most of them looked overpriced and overly fussy, determined to keep guests segregated from Actual California with an army of golf buggies, stand-alone villas and private butlers. I wanted to get California under my fingernails as soon as possible. So I booked us a Jucy campervan: a refitted Dodge van with a bed in the back and a small stove, which only cost us around $40 a day. This is a major saving in California, which has some of the most inflated hotel prices I've ever come across. For a travel writer, renting this campervan felt like true freedom: a trip I didn't need to write about! I mean, I could write about it later, if I felt like it (and this, right now, is me feeling like writing about California) but there was no style guide from the *Telegraph*'s hotel team to think about, no deadline from *Condé Nast Traveller*, no pressure from Visit California to Instagram every single brunch.

But before we gave ourselves over to nights in the van, under the redwoods, there was one hotel I needed to see. The Madonna Inn sits conveniently between Los Angeles and San Francisco, in the pleasant little town of San Luis Obispo, which was recently voted one of the best places to live in California. Such polls are normally meaningless, geared up really to boost property sales or give journalists something to write about. But SLO is a nice little spot, with a Wednesday night farmers' market where you can eat pulled pork and drink kombucha and mill around the main street to the sound of a jazz quartet. The Madonna Inn, though, is the main draw for tourists, a high temple to all things pink, kitsch and calorific. When you enter this supremely souped-up 1950s motel, a pink and white mock-Tudor ranch, you're immediately greeted by a bakery hawking pornographic-looking cupcakes. The decor is just as sugary. There are Barbie-pink tennis courts, a restaurant with hot pink banquettes and gilded chandeliers dangling from the ceiling, an opulent fountain in the men's urinals that male guests are encouraged to contribute to. Every room has a distinct, and wildly varied, theme, such as, 'Mountain Cabin', 'Austrian Suite', 'Pioneer America' and 'Irish Hills'. Essentially, every room is dedicated to a different sexual fantasy. Or 'interior design concept', if you prefer, because the whole point of interior design is to make people think about having sex in that particular room. On the pile rug or along the Chesterfield sofa? Over the Danish sideboard, or across the Norwegian leather armchair? Perhaps up against that industrial-chic exposed brickwork?

The interior design concept of our hotel was 'Kona Rock', a cave room, and as soon as we entered we felt the pressure. If you aren't having primal, caveman sex in Kona Rock within ten minutes of checking in, you are losers in life and love. Naturally, Sean and I did not have sex in that room.

It had been a long, uncomfortable flight from London, followed by a brief sleep and a long, sweaty drive from LA, and so minutes after dumping our bags in Kona Rock I was in my newly purchased California bikini. I urged Sean to do the same and come and join me up in the Madonna Inn's famous pink pool for cocktails. And he said, 'I haven't got any swimming trunks.'

There are moments in every relationship when one partner becomes a bellowing Neanderthal because their lover did not realise how important something was to them. It's fantasy again. Fantasy screws us up. Sean had no idea that for weeks, as I worked twelve-hour days in order to fund us both on this trip, I'd been visualising the delicious, Instagrammable moment when we both sank gratefully into the pink pool of the Madonna Inn and clinked cocktail glasses, toasting our forthcoming Californian adventure. This is why I'd bought my new bikini. It's why I'd booked the pricey cave room. Sean and I have a longstanding joke that since I plan every single detail of every single trip, all he has to do on holiday is show up at the airport with some spare pants in a bag. On this occasion he hadn't even really managed to do that.

'Who the FUCK comes to California and doesn't pack their swimsuit?' I shrieked, jumping around our cave in my bikini like, well, actually, quite like a cavewoman. I stormed off to the pool, snatching both of our Complimentary Welcome Cocktail! coupons. While I sank two Old Fashioneds in tandem and sulked in the pool, a terrified Sean scuttled off to the retail park across the freeway in search of a twenty-four-hour Walmart so he could buy some swimming trunks to placate his banshee bride and salvage his relationship. An hour later, he joined me. By then I was drunk, he was emotionally scarred and we were both jet-lagged, so we ate some crisps and fell asleep at 8.30 p.m. in our cave, smelling of chlorine and crisps and not, sadly, of hot caveman sex.

But it's okay! Because if you bugger up the 'bed' bit of a B&B, there is still 'breakfast'. Your stay can still be salvaged. We went to the diner and ordered huge platefuls of *huevos rancheros*. 'And will that be with eggs, or with egg beaters?' the waitress inquired, politely, as if this was a normal question. 'What's an egg beater?' I asked. 'Fake eggs, basically,' she said, faintly apologetically, as I gazed at her curiously.

This was the first moment I felt glaringly, nakedly, European in California. It was a novelty, because, in Britain, we feel hopelessly out-Europeaned by the French, Italians and Germans. But at the Madonna Inn, when that bored waitress described 'egg beaters' to me, I gave her that precise wrinkle-nosed look of disdainful incredulity that a French person gives a Brit when we say that we don't have time for lunch, thanks, we're just going to grab a sandwich and eat it at our desks. Or an Italian when you ask for milk in your coffee. Or a German, when you say you're sorry you're late, but the train was delayed.

We Brits need to travel to America to feel quaintly European, and there would be many more instances like this over the next few months. I try to recycle, buy organic and Fairtrade when I can afford it, and generally do my best for the planet, but I in no way considered myself a militant eco-warrior until I landed in LA, where Silver Lake hipsters happily buy six plastic bottles of green juice every day, drive everywhere alone in their own massive gas-guzzling tanks and blast air conditioning through their open-windowed houses. And where supposedly hipster, self-consciously bohemian cafés insist on giving you a glass of water and your coffee in a plastic cup. I took to bringing my own mug and water bottle everywhere, and growing faintly hysterical when they reached for the plastics. 'NO! Not more PLASTIC CUPS, I implore you! Behold, I come bearing my own vessels and gourds!' This, along with my insistence on walking, cycling, getting the Metro bus or Uber Pooling everywhere in LA, marked me out as a European oddball.

Anyway, we left the Madonna Inn without having had hot sex, which is the main point of the Madonna Inn, but we did eat big breakfasts and get some great shots for Instagram, which are the other two supplementary points of the Madonna Inn. Two out of three isn't bad, I suppose. And I would still put the Madonna Inn up there among my favourite hotels in the world. I'd particularly recommend it as an in-at-the-deep-end intro-duction to California: unashamedly outrageous and devoted to pleasure. The best place to shake off any European guilt, reserve, prudishness and good taste. Good taste can ruin a hotel just as surely as a snotty manager or bedbugs. Good taste gets boring, you see. All travel is a fling, and sometimes you just want to fool around with a pornographic cupcake, or perhaps even a fake egg.

There's a reason California is the birthplace of the road trip: the rewards of getting around have never been more brazen and obvious. California's outdoorsy charms basically do the can-can for you as soon as you push pedal to floor on the free-way. With Western-style frontier towns and other-worldly desert landscapes to the south-east, dense and dramatic ancient forest along the Pacific Coast Highway to the north, rustic surf towns and swathes of sandy beaches fringing the western coast, snow-topped mountains and granite peaks in the national parks of the interior, as well as a smattering of compelling and characterful cities across the state, California offers travellers an almost glut-tonous array of travel experiences in a compact area. I felt like I was snorting natural beauty, big fat lines of it, every time we set off in the campervan.

Over the next ten days, we drove north and norther, search-ing for big trees of varying dimensions. A quick guide to big trees: the inland giant redwoods of California (found in Sequoia National Park) are the fattest and therefore bulkiest trees in the world, almost cartoon-like in their proportions. But the world's tallest trees are the coast redwoods, making for woodland with such huge dimensions that all humans are rendered as tiny pixies. The precise location of the tallest tree in the world, Hyperion, is a closely protected secret, but its towering cousins are pretty formidable, too.

We were destined for the redwood-fringed coastal towns of Big Sur, Carmel and Monterey, which I, in all my literary dorkiness, knew inspired the writers John Steinbeck, Henry Miller and Robinson Jeffers. Few spots in this West Coast state loom as large in the Californian imagination as Big Sur, a raw and rugged stretch of coastline nestled between the craggy Santa Lucia Range and the pounding surf of the Pacific Ocean. There's no real town centre to Big Sur; instead, secluded luxury treehouses peep out of the redwoods and heavenly seafood restaurants cling to clifftops along iconic Highway 1 just north of Pfeiffer Big Sur State Park. Big Sur still exudes a bohemian, creative spirit, and draws in twenty-first-century hippies, privacy-craving celebrities and artists as well as hikers, bikers and surfers. But let's face it, it's only the loaded artists who can afford to stay there, of which there are only about seven, globally, at the last count, and one is about to be indicted on tax evasion charges. Still, peddling its own unique brand of barefoot luxury, Big Sur remains a magical and profoundly Californian wilderness hideaway, and if I won some sort of literary prize sponsored by the Devil, and could choose myself a writer's retreat anywhere on the planet, it would be a modernist wooden lodge high in the trees above Big Sur.

We found that we could only afford to dip briefly into Californian luxury, with occasional breakfasts in 1970s lodges like Deetjen's Big Sur Inn, and the odd glass of Sonoma Chardonnay at a clifftop bar like Nepenthe, but that was enough for me. I was happiest lying flat on a picnic bench, gazing up at the redwoods that themselves gazed up at the stars, sucking on cannabis sweeties and listening to Jefferson Airplane.

The redwoods at Humboldt Redwoods National Park were so soaring and dense that they create a sort of eerie permanent twilight at their feet, with just occasional slices of light breaking through the canopy to the campsite below. I'll never understand why it was in California that LSD was invented, because this place is trippy enough. Aberdeen, or Zurich, or perhaps Dallas would have been more likely birthplaces of hallucinogenic gorgeousness.

We drove further north, to find the Lost Coast. At a certain latitude north, brown metal bear-proof lockers began appearing next to our pitches at campsites, cheery reminders that there are massive beasts loitering nearby which may accidentally rip you apart in hot pursuit of the peanut butter sandwich in your backpack. It was kind of fun, stocking our little brown larder every night, apart from the nagging thought that I'd be clawed to pieces while trying to arrange my herbal teas in alphabetical order on the shelf.

From the coast we ventured inland, where the trees are fat, but less tall. I guess a women's magazine would call them 'curvy'. I loved Sequoia and Kings, national parks that people overlook in their desperate race to Yosemite. In spring, perhaps the smartest time to visit, the park's meadows are smeared in wildflowers, but in autumn we got toasted hues and golden evenings. Sequoia National Park is home to General Sherman, a giant sequoia which is the largest known living single stem tree on earth. Quite a claim. He's massive. And hanging out with him was brilliant, because we'd watch families from all over the world doing camera swapsies and laughing about the impossibility of capturing the tree's vastness in a single frame.

I could have watched people gathering at his roots all day. We obligingly took pictures of extended families from Tehran, retired couples from New Zealand and young friends from Germany, and everyone bonded over the sheer delight in this massive, massive tree. Sometimes the sightseers are more joyful to see than the sight itself.

When you're staring at a massive tree, everything slides into perspective. There's nothing like being put in your place by nature to make human beings realise what we all have in common. It occurred to me that if all international negotiations took place at the foot of General Sherman, the world would be a much peachier place right now.

Ten days after that storming row in a cave at the Madonna Inn, Sean and I rolled back into Los Angeles, to our little Airbnb bedsit in Echo Park. We were home, and it was all brand new and exciting, and LA is used to welcoming wide-eyed, over-excited dreamers to their temporary home. LA is a city where nobody laughs at your dreams. People have always brought their dreams to this city, dreams of fame or fortune, or love, or toned abs; whatever your dream, the city does not mock. This is LA's only real code of ethics, the city's only rule. And LA's refusal to sneer at a dream is intoxicating, especially for us Brits, who consider self-deprecation a national sport.

It used to be fashionable to throw shade at Los Angeles. Civilised people, it was snootily murmured, preferred the East Coast; LA was the sun-worshipping, superficial and star-struck little sister to cultured, classy New York. Dorothy Parker, New York's queen of the pithy one-liner, described LA as 'seventy-two suburbs in search of a city', although she lived there for years and rather liked it. But, hey, I wouldn't let that get in the way of a good one-liner, either.

At any rate, it's now widely accepted that Los Angeles, a city that has always welcomed artists, dreamers and eccentrics, is in the throes of a cultural and culinary resurgence, while New York is basically only affordable to bores. Musicians and artists who have been priced out of Brooklyn regrouped in the shabby-chic villas and dive bars of Silver Lake. Gallerists spied opportunity in the vast warehouse spaces of downtown LA's Arts District, opportunity they were three decades too late for in NYC's Chelsea. Freelance creatives, young entrepreneurs and bohemians were lured west by the promise of an easier, breezier lifestyle, grabbing their surfboards, yoga mats and MacBooks and congregating in Venice Beach, Topanga Canyon and Los Feliz.

Today LA has a reputation as a city that richly rewards her residents, but continues to confound visitors. As a sprawling, congested and notoriously unwalkable city of interconnected neighbourhoods with no distinct centre, Los Angeles represents a challenge, but the secret to loving LA is to live it like a local, abandoning tick-box tourism and instead focusing on a few key neighbourhoods, easily navigable by foot or Uber. As Angelenos say, if you find yourself not liking LA, just drive five more minutes. You might love the next neighbourhood along.

I had chosen Echo Park for a number of reasons, but mainly because I love neighbourhoods that are up and coming, rather than those that have upped and come all over the place. Angelenos tend to group together the triumvirate of East LA hipster hoods – Silver Lake, Echo Park and Los Feliz – because of their increasingly blurred geographical and social boundaries. Back in the 1970s, Silver Lake became the nexus of Los Angeles' gay leather subculture, but by 2000 it was thoroughly gentrified, and today the artists, musicians and creatives who made it a byword for cool have nudged east into Echo Park or Los Feliz, or further afield to Atwater Village or Highland Park. Quaint Los Feliz, by contrast, has lost none of its charm: a mishmash of glamorous hilltop villas, Arts and Crafts cottages and mid-century apartments. Of the three, lovely Echo Park sounded most like my beloved Hackney, and therefore I knew I'd slot into life in Echo Park with relative ease.

In Echo Park I loved the Mexican heritage, the crumbling buildings, the reservoir, the parklands and the proximity to downtown. But I also absolutely wanted my LA to be walkable. Everyone says that you can't do LA without a car, but that's bollocks as long as you don't mind the odd funny glance. I got by for six months on foot and Uber. Doing California car-free does, however, require careful planning. I am not really one of those travellers who leaves things to chance. I used maps and charts. I read every single review of every single viable listing on Airbnb, scanning the words of other travellers to see how easy they found it to walk around. I unashamedly Googled 'coolest café in Echo Park' and 'yoga Echo Park' and 'hiking trails in Echo Park' and finally zeroed in on a cute bedsit in Ewing Street, where I could walk to the bus stop on Sunset Boulevard in fifteen minutes, be on a running trail in Elysian Park in five minutes, be at yoga in ten and a swish freelance-friendly café in seven.

Our Airbnb hosts, Claudia and Ben, lived next door to us and became immediate friends. Claudia is a wickedly funny second-generation Korean from Indiana, her husband Ben a musician and sound engineer. They dated in high school, attended prom together, then buggered off in separate directions and dated or married other random people before finding each other again and getting hitched in their early thirties. Claudia introduced me to Korean spas, one of the best things about LA, and Korean beauty products, like a gloop called Oops My Lip! that stained your lips for seven hours. She also always knew the current dumpling hotspot. There is nothing about LA that Claudia does not know. As a picky, perfectionist travel psychopath myself, Claudia was a real find. We'd go shopping in Koreatown together, and I'd return with three fuchsia lipsticks, a cucumber face mask and some frozen durian.

For decades, Koreatown and downtown LA was a bit of a joke, and a rather grim one at that. With the city's financial beating heart nine miles north-west along Sunset Boulevard in the studios of Hollywood, this paltry smattering of skyscrapers and abandoned warehouses held little appeal, with city workers scarpering at 5 p.m. and leaving the streets to the sketchy inhabitants of Skid Row. But thanks to council-backed initiatives like Bringing Back Broadway, heritage buildings have been conserved and restored, most notably the Bradbury (which stars in the original *Blade Runner*), Orpheum and the United Artists Building, now the 182-room Ace Hotel. The gradual restoration of Broadway's theatrical buildings, along with dazzling new arrivals such as the Gehry-designed Walt Disney Concert Hall and the brand-spanking-new Broad, kick-started DTLA's (Downtown LA) renaissance, and the previously overlooked neighbourhoods of the Arts District and Koreatown are experiencing the most rapid development in the city.

When Sean's visa ran out at the three-month mark and he returned to the UK to start a job search in earnest, I stayed on in LA indefinitely, because I was getting a lot of work there and we needed all the money we could muster at the time. I visited Mattel HQ, home to Barbie, for the *Telegraph*. I researched DTLA's food scene for a neighbourhood guide in *Condé Nast Traveller*. I wrote about Korean beauty products for Refinery29 and had my hair dyed at a salon where they only accept blondes. And I tried out naked yoga for *Grazia*. I was having a blast, and writing great features, and I was in no way ready to leave. Claudia and I had shit to do.

I splurged on a ClassPass membership, because I feel you get a unique perspective on a new city through the sweat of its inhabitants. My classpass allowed me to go to virtually any exercise class or gym in town, and Claudia drove me to swanky spin classes and hot yoga. I wrote a feature for *Women's Health* magazine about Santa Monica, essentially a laboratory for all the newest and most innovative/gimmicky fitness trends, such as vertical climbing workouts and hot barre and hot weights. It's also home to the kookiest, such as Feet & Paws Fitness (yep, that's interval training for dogs plus owners). For decades the beach-fringed suburb of Santa Monica has attracted the most health-obsessed inhabitants of a health-obsessed city (Los Angeles) in a health-obsessed state (California). With 310 days of sunshine annually, miles of golden sands, a pounding surf and the hiking trails of the Santa Monica Mountains, it had become a popular resort town by the early twentieth century.

And as the beachfront district closest to Hollywood, it was destined to become the palm-fringed playground of choice for sporty starlets, bodybuilders, dancers and performers. During the 1970s Jane Fonda opened her aerobics studio on Main Street, future Olympian Carl Lewis trained at the Santa Monica Track Club and Arnold Schwarzenegger pumped iron at the weight-lifting mecca, Gold's Gym. Today it's where fitness trends and health fads are cooked up, sampled by a hungry but ruthlessly discerning public, and then either spat out unceremoniously or swallowed, savoured and given the coveted Santa Monica seal of approval. (The best of the batch eventually make it across the pond, and we Brits giddily embrace Soulcycle, Barry's Bootcamp and paleo granola as brand spanking new, when Santa Monica-ites are 'totally over' them and on to the next big thing.)

The Fonda-like 1970s aerobics queens are still in Santa Monica, a few decades and husbands later, but they've swapped calisthenics for cardio-barre, and the grapefruit diet for paleo. The changing-room demographic includes an echelon of taut-faced, oddly airbrushed-looking women with immaculate blow-dries, who might be forty-nine or sixty-nine. They wouldn't dream of showering in these communal facilities (in fact, a lot of gyms and exercise studios in LA don't even have showers), and simply sweep up their Jimmy Choo bags, collect their tiny dogs from outside and disappear into tinted-windowed SUVs parked at the front door. The semi-recognisable celebrities do the same. But in addition to the older, highly maintained So-Cal golden girls and the starry crowd, there are fitness-obsessed twenty-somethings working in tech companies in Santa Monica's newly christened 'Silicon Beach', who'll happily spunk their entire pay cheque on £9 maca smoothies and £20 Soulcycle classes. I realise that mine are the only pale thighs in the room. I'm also the only one with mismatched gym socks. The only one plopping my sweaty gear into a tatty plastic Sainsbury's bag, rather than a zip-lock 'stayfresh' compartment in a Lululemon tote. And the only one who sniggers when the woman tonging her hair starts ranting about how 'betrayed' she feels because her chiropractor has relocated to San Francisco.

Walking Santa Monica's 2nd Street, every other person is carting a yoga mat; most are wearing neon New Balances. Because what Rodeo Drive is to designer boutiques Santa Monica's 2nd Street is to designer workouts. But there's also old-school sport that started here and never, ever, went away: rollerblading, surfing, volleyball on the beach. Cycling the boardwalk, I pass agile female acrobats somersaulting on the gymnast rings next to the monkey bars and hoops of Muscle Beach, city-provided exercise equipment which drew stuntmen and acrobats way back in the 1930s. A few blocks away is the original Gold's Gym, the bodybuilding mecca opened in 1965 by Joe Gold, who pioneered modern weights equipment and beefed up the bodies of his protégés Arnold Schwarzenegger and Dave Draper.

After a week in Santa Monica, I returned gratefully to Echo Park, which, to my Hackney-acclimatised eyes, felt like normality. What I loved about Echo Park, and what I had actively sought out in a new neighbourhood for this six-month life swap with London, was the perfect mix of the reassuringly familiar urban tropes and the fiercely exotic reminders that I was on the other side of the planet to London. The yoga studios, bookshop cafés, street art and Wholefoods stores could have been in Hackney, but the dazzling sunsets over Sunset Boulevard (isn't it nice when names work?), the aroma of tacos, and even the fluorescent glare of the twenty-four-hour Walgreens pharmacy sign that marked my turn up Echo Park Boulevard, all reminded me that I was not in Kansas anymore.

LA was old and new to me at the same time, and that is how this vastly underrated city stole my heart. I found myself on a perpetual nostalgia trip in LA, because life in LA feels like living in a movie. This is because just about everywhere you go *has* actually been in a bloody movie. My local coffee shop, Valerie's, was always popping up in sitcoms. Echo Park Reservoir was in *Chinatown*. Kurt Vile's 'Pretty Pimpin' video gave such a thorough overview of Echo Park that I would send the YouTube link to people before they visited us, as an alternative to Google Maps. Our local diner, Bright Spot, was closed one morning while Christopher Walken and Al Pacino filmed a scene for *Stand Up Guys*. Every day in LA there are a hundred little moments that belong to the movies, as well as to you. It's fun to share things with the movies.

And you really, really do share LA with the movies. It's hard to overstate just how all-consuming the movie industry is in LA. In London, when I told people I was a writer, most assumed I was a journalist. In LA, there are about three journalists, and when you say 'writer', people think 'screenwriter'. 'Working on a feature' means working on a film here. And the conversations you overhear on the streets are all people jabbering about stuff being 'greenlit' or 'in development'. My ears soon became attuned to juicy conversations about celebrities, because suddenly the tone would turn uniformly reverential, and 'the talent' would be referred to by first name only: 'Leo' or 'Emma' or 'Margot'.

LA has the highest calibre Uber drivers in the world, because they are all out of work actors or scriptwriters between seasons. Nobody waits tables or turns tricks anymore. And most Airbnbs, ours included, are a second income for people vaguely attached to the biz. The sharing economy – Uber, Airbnb, TaskRabbit – has been a very, very good thing for a city built on that fickle heartbreaker of an industry, show business.

And before you know it, living in LA you are friends with actors. You can't avoid actors, although it's worth trying. My lovely writer friend Dawn O'Porter is married to an Irish actor, and at Sunday barbecues at their place in West Hollywood I'd be that embarrassing Brit who was *sure* I'd met someone before, until Dawn would mercifully step in and say, 'Jack was in *30 Rock*, so you probably know him from that, and not a party in Shoreditch, hon'. Through Dawn and Chris I met virtually every Irish person working in Hollywood, and the Irish, it turns out, are a potent force in Hollywood. But they were still brilliantly Irish, complaining about the weather being too hot, going boogie-boarding in Malibu in their pants to get rid of post-awards hangovers, and getting rip-roaringly drunk at every available opportunity.

And my Irish buds sympathised when I told them my tale of karaoke woe after Claudia's birthday. I turned up to karaoke late, obviously, and a little bit drunk, obviously, because this is karaoke. Claudia's mainly gay and mainly showbiz friends took karaoke seriously; they'd brought costumes, props, they each had their own choreographed routine for the song they whipped out at every single karaoke session. And they weren't drunk. In LA, not-singing is a lost art. Everyone performs. All the time.

I knew, right away, that whatever tune I sang I was essentially performing a roly-poly alongside the Russian gymnastics team at the 1988 Olympics. I hurriedly chose 'My Sharona' by The Knack as, I thought, a pretty safe belt-it-out one-hit-wonder. It was only when I stood up and began singing that I realised this was one of those songs that was an unquestioned hit at the time, but is now somewhat marred by creepy lyrics. 'Such a dirty mind/I always get it up, for the touch of the younger kind,' I sang, miserably, feeling so drunk and so Irish.

HOW TO WIN AT JET LAG

If I'm travelling long haul, I do something totally hardcore to dodge jet lag. I don't eat anything at the airport or on the plane, and only eat again when it's breakfast in my destination country. Yes, I get bloody hungry. Yes, it takes discipline. Yes, it's boring and joyless. But it's a lot less joyless than spending the first five days in a new destination feeling nauseous and knackered, and, after one particularly gnarly transition from LA time to London time, I vowed to do this instead.

This regime is loosely based on the Argonne Anti-Jet Lag diet, invented by scientist Charles Ehret, who found that our biological clocks and circadian rhythms are partially ▶

239

determined by our stomachs. Ehret discovered that irregularly timed meals of varying size and composition 'gradually unmoored' the body's biological clock, and the Argonne diet has been used to great effect by the army, navy, the CIA and sports teams. The full-on diet requires multiple days of feasting and fasting, which I don't have time for. The simpler but tougher version is this: establish breakfast time at your destination – say 8 a.m. – and then fast for twelve hours before that time. Nothing but water. I know. When it's 8 a.m. in your destination time zone, hoover up breakfast like you've never seen a breakfast before. Obviously this is way easier on overnight flights, which would always be my preference for long-haul journeys.

Despite the odd karaoke humiliation or hippy meltdown in a café when they tried to give me a plastic cup, I sank into my new LA routine with ease. I've always loved building new routines in new places. I brought my London mindset with me to LA, and one of the most glaring ways this manifested itself was that I thought nothing of sitting on the bus for an hour, cruising up Sunset Boulevard to Soho House in West Hollywood.

While most Angelenos shudder at the thought of Hollywood's more touristy offerings, like the celebrity handprints outside the Chinese Theatre and the studio tours, West Hollywood (or WeHo) has retained its cool credentials, thanks largely to the vibrant gay community (as of 2013, 39 per cent of WeHo's residents are gay men), vegan restaurants and Museum Row: five museums (most notably Los Angeles County Museum of Art, or LACMA) within walking distance of each other. Sunday is Funday in WeHo; it's all bottomless mimosas over brunch, tipsy shopping at The Grove, and drag queen bingo at Hamburger Mary's. Gayness has saved West Hollywood; if gayness didn't exist, WeHo would be crap.

I'd been using Soho House in Shoreditch as my gym/workspace/pub for years, and I saw no reason to change this habit now I was in LA. So I'd cheerfully step off the bus in West Hollywood, walk through the car park to the front door (there was no pedestrian entrance, there being no pedestrians in LA apart from me), past celebrities being valeted and ushered in along a red carpet, then set up my laptop next to Mila Kunis or Harry Styles, order the cheapest thing on the menu and start typing. I could get away with this, I think, because I was that eccentric European girl, the one who *gets the bus from Echo Park*, who knows all the bar staff by name, and who insists on taking a few moments out to watch the sun sink into the Pacific at six o'clock every evening.

It was this intermingling of the familiar and the seductively new that attracted me most about LA. LA shares some of London's finest urban qualities, but LA was dressed up in glamorous, sexy garb. LA had hummingbirds that hovered next to my laptop as I sat, typing away, on my porch. LA had such year-round balmy weather that coats are really just for fun, purely decorative. And LA has magical, magical light. The reason that studio bosses set up here was because of the reliably glorious light. Sunlight is a presence in itself in LA; you wake up and you're with the light, and you and the light hang out all day together until it leaves you in the evening, and you feel bereft but also slightly liberated and you have to have a drink to wind down from such a heady day with the light.

And, gradually, LA felt more and more like a serious relationship, while London felt like a beloved but ultimately bloody hard work ex-lover. So when I got that call, as I sat gazing at a hummingbird above my laptop on Claudia's porch in Echo Park, that call from Sean telling me he'd got a job in London, that I could come home now, that he'd find us a flat in west London, I felt my heart break a little bit. And as I travelled to the airport a few days later, listening to The Smiths and dreaming of getting aboard that Virgin Atlantic flight and sinking a few red wines, I told LA that I'd be back. That I loved her, that we really did have something special here. That London meant nothing to me by comparison. And this time, I really meant it.

13

Margate: Finding Home

When you leave a city as spectacular as Los Angeles, you'd better have a plan. A good one. I, sadly, did not have a good plan, and I came back down to earth, in Britain, with a rough old bump. My husband Sean had got a job, very much the job of his dreams, at the Royal Horticultural Society HQ in Wisley, out in Surrey, very much the place of my nightmares. We looked into renting a flat in west London, realising we just couldn't afford it on a combined gardener/freelance writer salary, and then Sean snapped and took a short-term rental out in Surrey, in a housing development between Walton-on-Thames and Weybridge. This was far not only from my beloved Hackney, but far beyond my sacred Zone 2, beyond Zone 6 even. It was the suburbs, suburbs unsweetened by most of the promises of the burbs: a larger home with a garden (we were still in a one-bed flat), cheaper rent (it cost pretty much the same as Hackney) or lovely views (more identikit pebbledash homes). Surrey, I realised, was my travel kryptonite, the one place I couldn't crack, couldn't uncover a sliver of charm in. I found Surrey harrowing.

I lasted thirty-six hours, although I cried for thirty of them. The first six hours I spent optimistically walking the half-hour into both Weybridge and Walton-on-Thames, in search of some sort of redeeming feature, or even a decent café I could take my laptop to tomorrow to escape the misery flat. I found a Phase Eight, a Slug and Lettuce, a couple of miserable Costa cafés, and a lot of miserable inhabitants. Because this wasn't even posh Surrey. This was middle-ranking Surrey; furious bankers who felt underappreciated and underpaid, and their equally bitter wives. Chain restaurants, chain cafés, expensive beauty salons, car showrooms and estate agents. There was nothing in Surrey for me at all, nothing to do but wait for Sean to get home. And he would be grumpy, because he'd had a bad drive because everyone in Surrey drives as aggressively as Jeremy Clarkson when he really, really needs a piss. I think this is when I started to cry.

My strong allergic reaction to Surrey surprised me, and not just because it's my job, really, to travel somewhere new and find the charm, the beating heart, the thing that makes it tick. Getting to grips with unfamiliar and seemingly inhospitable surroundings, well, I'm used to ticking that box before I sit down for breakfast. But also because the violence of my reaction felt almost primal, as if my very essence was under threat, somehow. And I can only surmise, based on a rudimentary knowledge of popular psychology accrued over a twelve-year career in magazines, that at some point in my life I've come across lives of suburban drear, and silently vowed to myself that this would never, ever happen to me. Yet now – Abrakebabra! – I found myself living in my worst nightmare, just days after leaving my dreamy existence in LA.

And Sean and I had not quite had the passionate reunion that I'd hoped for. We'd been living separate lives for the past three months, he chucking himself into the study of horticulture, and mountain-biking, and me getting drunk with actors in Soho House West Hollywood and writing about naked yoga. Now, as he prepared for a job he'd happily be in for life, in a place I couldn't stand to be in for more than thirty-six hours, the differences between us seemed as wide as the Atlantic. In this book, if Sean seems like a background character, that's because he'd become one in my life. I hadn't put him there. He'd retreated, slipped backstage, and stopped joining me at social occasions, or accompanying me on short trips away.

For years, I'd been using the words 'I just need to get away' to describe my craving for a trip. Now I wondered if the words 'I'm running away!' would have been more honest. Sometimes when we need a change, the real change we need is inside us. I've always justified my constant travel by summoning images of freedom, experience and adventure. Not denial and cowardice. I sell travel to people, through my words, on MacBook screens and printed pages. Good salespeople make very good self-delusionists.

I'd married a wonderful, wonderful man, but everyone knew we were wildly different characters. And now, I wasn't sure I was a force for good in his life anymore. I felt like something he depended upon without really thinking about. I felt like baggage.

And I felt that, as he embarked upon an exciting new career, a demanding, city-loving, itchy-footed and action-obsessed wife who didn't really care about plants and couldn't handle living in Surrey was the last thing he needed. And, yes, I began to wonder what my life would be like if I was solo in life, like I was solo on my travels. When I thought about it, I realised that every extended trip we'd taken together had been instigated by me – and ended by Sean. Would I return to LA? Perhaps New Zealand? And if I'm being really honest, every trip was my attempt to fix our relationship somehow. Every trip was a failed attempt to make Sean happy, so he would treat me as if he loved me. I'd been trying and failing for years, and the constant hope – and constant failure – was wearing me down. In that flat in Surrey, with nothing to distract me from the problems in my relationship, I realised that this very hope was ruining my life, and I was through with it.

This was a fairly devastating realisation, and all the angry Surrey drivers and identikit suburban houses were not improving my state of mind, so I tearfully packed my rucksack and went off to stay with my gloriously understanding and ferociously loyal cousin, Kathryn, who always finds the time to cook up coq au vin for her hobo Irish relation every time I'm in a jam.

I'd just pulled the rug out from underneath my life, and tossed everything up in the air. I knew I'd potentially scuppered my relationship with Sean by failing to be a supportive partner while he embarked upon this exciting new career path. I'd just left a home I liked, in LA, and I considered hopping on the next Virgin Atlantic flight back, but my little Airbnb bedsit was booked for months now by some bloody writer for *Orange Is the*

New Black that Claudia, that heartbreaker, was already taking for dumplings and watching *RuPaul's Drag Race* with.

To distract myself from my imminent mid-thirties crisis, I dispatched myself to the Kentish seaside town of Margate, to write about the grand reopening of Dreamland, Britain's oldest amusement park, for *Stylist* magazine. For centuries, Margate was one of the grandest resort towns in England. Royalty, aristocrats and artists holidayed here, spending weeks at grand Georgian townhouses, shopping at the likes of Russell & Bromley (now a charity shop) and spending days at the vast 1,000-capacity Lido Sands, with dance halls, outdoor pools and cocktail bars.

I was fascinated. The best thing about being a writer is having carte blanche to be both pushy and nosy, and I spent my weekend grilling residents old and new about their favourite spots and reasons for being in Margate – and gratefully accepting generous invitations to beach picnics at Botany Bay, art exhibitions at Handverk and Found, impromptu parties at Cheesy Tiger on the harbour arm, and shrieking, gleeful dips in the sea.

My friend Gemma Cairney, a writer and radio broadcaster, was DJing at the Dreamland launch party that night, and she told me she'd bought a flat in Margate a few months earlier, the very first weekend she visited, because she just bloody loved the place. I cannot imagine a more enthusiastic tour guide. And something happened to me, something I've half-expected on every single work trip I ever set off on. Margate stopped feeling like a travel story, and started feeling like a potential home. Within days, I was staying at Gemma's Airbnb in Margate, still living out of the rucksack I'd escaped Surrey with.

I should clarify that I use the word 'home' loosely, the way advocates of free love might mention their current lover. Margate might be my home for a few months, or a few years, who knows – home, like love, was a nebulous concept to me, more a state of mind than a time commitment. Those extended working trips to New Zealand, Bali and LA had all broken London's decade-long spell over me, my options had opened up wide and I felt adventurous again. I didn't actually need to live in London, I realised, I just needed to be able to get into the city a couple of times a week. And I figured that if I was going to be in limbo, I might as well be somewhere where every day life felt like a holiday.

Also, my priorities had been reshuffled by the past three years of travel, as *Stylist*'s travel editor. New Zealand had taught me that I wanted a more outdoorsy lifestyle, ideally at the beach. In Detroit, I'd seen young people like me buying and fixing up their own homes, and I dreamed of owning my own flat, a flat that could handle a cat. The user-friendliness of a city like Glasgow had made me intolerant of London's lengthy commutes and sky-high rents, which I'd come to see as the enemy of creativity. I was never going to be able to take a gamble, and take a few months off paid commissions to write a book (this book), while I was frantically typing away, like a muppet at a piano, to scrape together the rent each month. I will always love London, and I owe the city a lot. My career as a writer is the greatest gift I've ever been given, and London gave me my career. But the other cities I'd seen, well, they'd made me realise there was more to life than London.

My first Monday morning at Gemma's Airbnb in Margate I

woke up at six o'clock out of sheer excitement, saw the sunshine hit the sea through those huge bay windows and hopped on my bike to wind my way around the Kentish coast to Ramsgate. In London, a forty-five-minute cycle took me from Walthamstow to Clerkenwell, through industrial estates and along fume-choked streets. Here it took me past white cliffs, melodramatic cliff-hugging castles, country pubs and increasingly deserted sandy beaches, like scenes from a Daphne du Maurier novel. I was at my laptop and working by 9 a.m., but I'd already had an adventure before breakfast.

One fuzzy Sunday morning, dared by Gemma, I leapt into Margate's Grade II Listed tidal pool. I'd hoped for nothing more than a hangover cure; I found a life-changing habit. Every morning I'd walk along the beach to the tidal pool and swim eight lengths, and I'd leave the sea knowing that, whatever happened, everything would be okay. The sea does that to me. The coldness of the water numbed and soothed my hot little head, rinsing away any residual stress and unnecessary worries. The saltiness stung my nostrils, and awakened my senses, and I emerged from the water feeling reborn. And the sheer beauty of the sea, wavy horizontal lines and blueness all around me, pushed inconsequential thoughts from my mind and gave me hope again. Not the desperate, unrealised, soul-crushing hope I associated with my marriage, but a general sense that things are going to be okay after all.

The sea was a major upgrade from running around the streets of Dalston and swimming the crowded, chlorinated swimming lanes of Clissold Leisure Centre. I made a lot of friends in the tidal pool, and when you meet someone wet and cold and essentially in your pants, there's no room for airs or graces or any element of standoffishness.

During my swims at Walpole Bay Tidal Pool, I became fascinated by the demographic soup I was part of in Margate: along with the growing community of Londoners, like me, who've ditched the city for the seaside, I met Polish grandmothers, Nigerian families, Romany teenagers and Kentish schoolboys. There's no greater social leveller than cold water; stripped of our clothing and other social props, we're all reduced to small, shivering, fragile humans. As one Polish grandmother said to me, in broken and beautiful English, 'We are all sea friends here.'

I found Margate friendly on dry land as well as in the sea. I guess I've always been a bit addicted to the thrill of mastering new surroundings – waking up in a new, alien city and somehow making it my own. And I've succeeded everywhere, except Surrey. It's this thirst for challenge and novelty that kept me on the road for so long. In Margate, all the newcomers like me are keen to make friends, so there's a perennial – and occasionally dangerous – Freshers' Week vibe. And there's no space for snobbery in such a small town. If you're a dick to someone, you'll see them seven times the same day, and frankly that gets awkward. I quickly felt my Northern Irish manners being reinstated in their rightful place, after years being dislodged by the anonymity of a big city like London.

I decided to extend my stay, and rented a flat in Hawley Square that belonged to James Brown, the launch editor of *Loaded*, and a media name that had been seared into my soul from the age of fourteen. When I told travel writer friends that after three years of virtually non-stop travel I was finally settling down, I was generally greeted with looks of abject horror. Every travel writer expects that, one day, they'll lose their hearts and minds to a destination, and stay there for eternity. But most of them picture Florence, Gstaad or Tulum. Not Margate, one of Britain's most notoriously rundown seaside resorts.

When my beloved Walpole Bay Tidal Pool was built in 1937, alongside an extravagant art deco funicular railway elevator linking the genteel mansion hotels of Cliftonville with the promenade below, Margate was one of the grandest resort towns in England. But when package tourism took off in the 1970s and British holidaymakers buggered off to France and Spain, these grand hotels and B&Bs were carved up into cheap accommodation. A large number of homeless and vulnerable people were moved into the area; this decision made Margate's fall from grace more painful and humiliating than that of rival seaside towns. As a Margate Renewal study carried out by Thanet council in 2007 put it, 'Margate Central contains just 41% owner-occupied housing, compared to a district and national average of around 70%, and a correspondingly high proportion of private rented stock. Vulnerable adults, ex-offenders and asylum seekers are placed in the wards in higher numbers than anywhere else in the County, and are often isolated, and far from home.'

As a result, Margate's demographic, particularly in Cliftonville, has changed dramatically over the last few decades. In 2011 unemployment in the town stood at about 20 per cent, with the highest number of people on benefits in the entire country. A few streets away from the tidal pool is Dalby Square, home to the highest proportion of unemployed residents in the UK. At one reckoning, one in three residents is on Jobseekers' Allowance. This has all helped to create tension in the community, amounting to widespread support for UKIP, who campaigned heavily in the area in the 2017 general election.

Phwoar, I thought, as I read crime reports and delved into bleak socioeconomic surveys. None of this put me off Margate. Years of travel have taught me that all the most interesting destinations have had a bit of a rough ride, socio-economically, and possess a complex character to show for it. I shouldn't be glib about the challenges facing Margate's council and social services, or the levels of deprivation in the streets that surround my flat in Cliftonville. But people have been down on Margate for decades, shaking their heads and muttering that Margate isn't 'home material'. Screw them, I say. I fancied the fuck out of Margate from the moment I met her. Margate was the opposite of Surrey.

RESPONSIBLE TRAVEL

We have to face facts: travelling is not a particularly ecologically sound pursuit, and in many destinations, tourism is mismanaged which heaps issues of social injustice, cultural friction and economic marginalisation on top of the environmental factors. However, I fully believe that travel *can* be a force for good. I believe that a thoughtful traveller can distribute much-needed income into local communities and foster bonds between different nationalities. The tourism industry can be a valuable incentive for local governments to preserve local traditions and prioritise areas of natural beauty and heritage buildings — because when good sense, community spirit and integrity fail lawmakers, cold hard cash often does the trick. But for tourism to be a positive force, rather than contributing to a destination's problems, it requires us all to think long and hard about how, where and why we spend our travel buck. Below are some rules I follow.

Opt for independent hotels, cafes, restaurants and stores wherever possible. Sure, it's tempting to pop into the familiarity of a Tesco in Surat Thani in Thailand, but the local shops deserve your custom more. There is nothing sadder to me than gated multinational resorts with private beaches, where every pound a traveller spends goes straight into the pocket of a Swiss owner, and nothing filters through to the local community, who have had their livelihoods threatened by the mass occupation of the coastline.

Choose local tour operators rather than multi-national operators, which tend to be US- or European-owned.

Travel by public transport wherever possible. This is also much, much more fun — I always feel like travelling by private transfer or taxi means missing out on a valuable cultural experience. It's a wasted opportunity.

▶

There's no escaping the ecological impact of air travel, so at least treat air travel with the respect it deserves. I try to avoid domestic flights and opt for rail instead. These days I travel to fewer destinations, but stay for a longer time, reducing the flight:trip ratio favourably.

Do think twice about luxury hotels. For a long time luxury was synonymous with waste and excess: vast overheated spa areas, exotic foods flown in from across the globe, towels and bed linen washed after a single use, countless tiny plastic bottles of water, shampoo and Gordon's gin consumed. Look into a hotel's eco credentials through a company like Bouteco.co, or choose a simpler place to stay, rather than supporting the excesses of the luxury tourism sector.

Visit sites such as packforapurpose.org and stuffyourrucksack. wordpress.com to find out how you can distribute school or medical supplies to remote destinations.

Have some respect. Speak a few words of the local language, dress in a manner that is culturally appropriate, don't get shit-faced, don't assume every taxi driver/waiter/guide is out to shaft you, and tell people how much you appreciate being in their country. You really are an ambassador, so don't be a crap one.

Cut down on plastics. I travel with a LifeStraw water filter so I never need to consume plastic water bottles on the go, and I only nick hotel toiletries when I really need them.

Think about your destination, too – perhaps visit a lesser-known city to spread the love (and wealth) a bit, visit in low season to take less of a toll on the environment and support local industry through a fallow period, and refuse to rule out destinations that have just been hit by flooding or violence. Destinations being abandoned wholesale because of news headlines is financially disastrous for the local community. When it's safe to do so, the most responsible approach is to continue to support the local travel industry.

Margate was a mishmash of all my favourite destinations, an irresistible cocktail of grit and grandeur, hope and gloom, practicality and eccentricity. This Victorian seaside town had the grandeur of Bath or Edinburgh, but it was a sexy, dishevelled grandeur, like Helena Bonham Carter in a ripped prom dress in *Fight Club*. I've always felt that 'faded' is my favourite flavour of grandeur, anyway. Margate also had the dreamy, beachy vibe of a Santa Monica or Auckland – minus the crowds, the smugness and the towering skyscrapers. Margate has just one skyscraper, the much-maligned Arlington House, built in 1964 as a dazzling white pillar to space-age optimism, now a gloriously retro Brutalist vision of the future. And Margate had the gritty optimism of a city that has been through some shitty times, like Detroit, Budapest or Belfast. When I visited Detroit it struck me as one of the world's most optimistic cities – a city where things hit rock bottom, but now a positive, plucky, pioneer spirit prevails. In Margate, as in Detroit, young people can afford their dreams, be it a family home for £100,000, their own furniture store, a recording studio, a writer's den moments from the beach, or a yoga studio. Margate is a generous hostess. She's been hosting visitors for centuries, you see.

I was first attracted to Margate by her beaches, but what made me stick around was the people I met here, the glorious eccentricity of the local community, and the melodramatic social history. The tragic tale of this eager-to-please Victorian tart-with-a-heart being cruelly forsaken by fickle tourists seduced by Spanish resorts like Torremolinos and Malaga and left to rot for decades was irresistible to me. Tourism made Margate, then it broke her, and the Margate we are all building today is one for the residents, the lifers, not the tourists.

And, amazingly, I was able to become a resident. I found a little £129,000 one-bedroom flat in Cliftonville that I could afford to buy, in a building that used to be a school. It's on the ground floor, so cat-flap friendly, and it's a five-minute walk from the tidal pool, so I can walk home after a swim in my costume and a towel, if I feel shameless enough, which I always do. My flat is small, but it's beautiful, and it's mine. It's so lovely, with high ceilings and a huge fireplace, that when I moved in I felt that I should only listen to opera music here, that classical music was the only fitting soundtrack to such a lovely space. But obviously I got over that, and these days I blare Nick Cave, Pavement, The Pixies, Kate Bush and Led Zeppelin as I get ready for yoga in the morning.

I guess there's a delicious irony in it being a resort town that finally persuaded me to settle down, because Margate is a place where every day feels a bit like a holiday. I learned that a lot of the things I thought I had to travel abroad for – sunny afternoons on the beach, salty plunges in the sea, the simpler routine of life in a small town, a deliciously carefree aura – could be found here in Britain, and now on my doorstep. Much of my urge to travel was a desire to reconnect with nature and live a simpler life. But I don't want to need trips. I want to want trips, unlike the Wichita lineman.

After years of non-stop travel, nothing seems more exotic to me than familiarity: knowing my postman by name, volunteering in the local Oasis charity shop and putting down roots. I've always been good at making new friends on my travels, but it means a whole lot more when you get to keep these friends, get to know them better and better on the beach and at picnics, until finally you realise you both care and will do really annoying tasks for each other like carrying a futon down the street or flyering for their club night.

It feels brave, too, to be setting up a home on my own. I feel bolder today than I did gorilla-tracking in Rwanda, driving the ice roads in the Canadian Arctic, or doing a loop-the-loop in a Tiger Moth over New Zealand. I'd become very, very good at paying attention to my external surroundings, at rendering my environment into words, at digging deep and seeing what other people don't in a destination. I'd been so busy gazing at the outside world that I'd failed to see what was happening inside, or perhaps I'd been too afraid to look. Now that I've hit the pause button, my adventuring is all inside me. This inner adventure is proving just as transformative as those months backpacking around South East Asia.

In many ways, hanging up my rucksack and settling down

with Margate is the greatest adventure I've had in years. I still don't know what's going to happen to my love life, I don't know if I'll ever have a family, or ever get that cat. But I know that, after a lifetime of departures, I hope I'm ready to arrive.

Acknowledgements

I'd like to thank my agent, Becky Thomas, for believing in this book right away. And Rhiannon Smith, my editor at Little, Brown, for letting me write the book I wanted to write and generously reassuring me that yes, my jokes are funny. Most of the time.

Departures would not exist without the support, good humour, perfectly-judged criticism and endless patience of my editors over the years: Mike Peake and Ross Brown at *FHM*, *Suzy Cox* and Victoria Harper at *Grazia*, Lisa Smosarski and Susan Riley at *Stylist*, Fiona Kerr at *Conde Nast Traveller*, Jane Bruton, Kate Bussmann, Marianne Jones and Claire Irvin at *The Daily Telegraph*, Jade Beer, Claudia Waterson and Harriet Jones at *Conde Nast Brides*, Farrah Storr and Amy Grier at *Cosmopolitan*, Juliet Kinsman at Smith Hotels, Hannah Marriott at *The Guardian*, Serena Guen, Olivia Squire and India Dowley at *Suitcase* and anyone who has ever fired off an email on a dull grey morning and dispatched me on a life-changing adventure. I hope you know who you are.

Lastly I'd like to think every fellow traveller I've shared an airline seat, beer or sunset with. I learned something from every single one of you.